Dedication

To all those who have picked up the towel and basin
and made a difference in their communities.
We applaud you and thank you for the inspiration
and for the many stories you've shared with us,
a few of which have found their way to these pages.

—Eric and Rick

THE
EXTERNALLY FOCUSED CHURCH

RICK RUSAW & ERIC SWANSON

Foreword by Robert Lewis

Loveland, Colorado

Group resources actually work!

This Group resource incorporates our R.E.A.L. approach to ministry. It reinforces a growing friendship with Jesus, encourages long-term learning, and results in life transformation, because it's

Relational
Learner-to-learner interaction enhances learning and builds Christian friendships.

Experiential
What learners experience through discussion and action sticks with them up to 9 times longer than what they simply hear or read.

Applicable
The aim of Christian education is to equip learners to be both hearers and doers of God's Word.

Learner-based
Learners understand and retain more when the learning process takes into consideration how they learn best.

Credits
Senior Acquisitions Editor: Brian Proffit
Chief Creative Officer: Joani Schultz
Editor: Candace McMahan
Copy Editor: Linda Marcinkowski
Art Director and Print Production Artist: Dana Scherrer, idesignetc
Cover Art Director: Jeff A. Storm
Cover Designer: Toolbox Creative
Cover Photographer: Daniel Treat
Production Manager: Peggy Naylor

Library of Congress Cataloging-in-Publication Data
Rusaw, Rick, 1959-
The externally focused church / by Rick Rusaw and Eric
Swanson.--1st American pbk. ed.
    p. cm.
  Includes bibliographical references.
  ISBN 978-0-7644-2740-4 (pbk. : alk. paper)
1. Christianity--United States. 2. Church. I. Swanson, Eric, 1950- II. Title.
  BR515.R96 2004
  261--dc22

                                     2004005822

20 19 18 17 16 15 14 13 12 11   13 12 11 10 09 08
Printed in the United States of America.

Table of Contents

Foreword

Something wonderful is happening today. After a long slumber, the evangelical church is reawakening to its *other side*. I call it the *proof* side of proclaiming the gospel.

I first experienced this other side when our church, along with several others, organized to renovate some of the public schools in our area. Teachers and school officials had not asked for our help and were clearly surprised when we offered it. But when thousands of church volunteers descended on their schools, rebuilding playgrounds, landscaping entryways, laying carpet, constructing hundreds of much needed cabinets, and painting hallways and classrooms, something special took place.

They believed…

Through witnessing these selfless demonstrations of love and helpful acts of service, they believed that the church just might have something worth listening to. I will never forget the comment of one fourth-grade teacher as she stood there, amazed at the work being done on her classroom by complete strangers: "If this is Christianity, then I'm interested," she said.

It was then and there that I realized our world is still open to a gospel it can hear *and see*. The real gospel is two-sided—it's *truth* and *proof*!

Imagine Jesus going out into towns and villages during his public ministry and proclaiming his gospel *without* accompanying acts of healing and helping (Matthew 9:35). Do we really think our Savior would have gained a hearing (much less a following) or established the credibility of his message—without displaying some proof that this gospel was real? *Why would we ignore such a model?*

We need to be like Jesus. Like him, we need to be *out* in our communities, connecting with people through acts of amazing love…while connecting *them* to a God of amazing grace. Now that's good news!

History tells us the church has always been at its best when its gospel comes two-sided like this. Evangelicals have had some of their greatest moments when this has been the case. One has to look back only a few years to John and Charles Wesley, William Wilberforce, and Charles Finney for some outstanding examples. But new examples are already on the horizon as more and more churches rediscover this external focus.

I have been overwhelmed with the response of our church since those early days when we took our first cautious steps into some of the urban neighborhoods of our city. Formerly passive church members have gained a new vision and energy for the use of their talents and gifts. New partnerships and friendships have been established. We no longer appear as some "secret society" or stranger to our city. We are now solidly networked all over our community. Today we have six full-time staff members devoted to enhancing and expanding our community strategy. Presently, we are thrilled to be beginning a multi-year project of adopting a130-block area of our city for social, spiritual, economic, and educational revitalization.

So if you're not already awake to what's happening today, I can assure you Eric Swanson and Rick Rusaw will get you there. These are good men with great insight regarding the sacred balance of truth and proof so needed in today's churches.

Through consulting with churches across America, Eric has a solid grasp on how God is right now turning a first wave of churches outward. You will be inspired, as I have been, by the real-life stories of the churches he describes in this book. As a practitioner, Rick has real-world, frontline experience in leading his church in learning how to connect with the community. Together in *The Externally Focused Church,* they offer a rich blend of scriptural insights, assessment perspectives, and practical how-to's that will energize you and lead you to rejoice over this current reawakening that's full of new opportunities and new adventures in transforming our world with the good news of Jesus Christ.

So sit back, relax, and let these men show you some of the "new things" God is doing in our world today.

—**Robert Lewis**
Founding Pastor, Fellowship Bible Church
Little Rock, Arkansas
Author, *The Church of Irresistible Influence*

Preface

When we first met three years ago, we recognized that each of us brings unique passions, contributions, and experiences to the subject of the externally focused church. Eric lives in Boulder, Colorado, and works with the Leadership Network as the director of Leadership Communities for Externally Focused Churches. He also serves as a consultant with CitiReach International, working with externally focused churches in several cities around the world. As the senior pastor of LifeBridge Christian Church in Longmont, Colorado, Rick is a pragmatic practitioner who has defined his thinking and passion for community engagement through his preaching, teaching, and writing. And in his role as an independent consultant, Rick has helped a number of people in leadership (in both business and ministry arenas) communicate and live out the vision God has given them. The result is that LifeBridge is a recognized leader among growing, externally focused churches.

Eric's thinking on constructs and models has helped Rick explain what he has practiced for years. And as Eric began identifying and investigating the emerging leaders of externally focused churches, he found himself telling the LifeBridge story wherever his travels took him. So for some time, we've benefited from each other's strengths and experiences.

This book is the tangible manifestation of that ongoing collaboration. It is intended to challenge pastors and church leaders to share the vision of being externally focused. At the end of each chapter, you'll find something to think about, something to talk about, something to act upon, and sermon or lesson ideas. We encourage you to reflect privately on these sections and then to share them with others to fuel their passion and vision for outreach and service.

In the "Closer Look" sections of the book (marked by a binocular icon), you'll find examples of externally focused churches in action or community agencies from which you can learn. Use these sections when you're looking for a quick illustration of the book's ideas while sharing them with other leaders in your church.

Co-writing a book is much like melding two useful objects in order to create something more useful and valuable than either could be by itself. Copper and zinc are heated to create brass, two streams converge to make a river, a man and woman recite vows to begin a marriage, hydrogen and oxygen molecules bond together to form water, and bacon and eggs make breakfast. Two distinct objects become useful as a third object by means of heat, pressure, time, or thoughtful design. We would like to thank Krista Petty, who through heat, pressure, and thoughtful design, extracted concept from chaos and clarity from ambiguity and, in the process, helped create something of greater value. Bacon and eggs take a cook to make breakfast. Paint and canvas need an artist to create a painting. Krista is that chef. Krista is that artist.

We would also like to thank our editor, Candace McMahan, whose meticulous attention to detail, accuracy, and continuity has helped us immeasurably in writing a book that will be useful to the body of Christ.

Finally, we wish to thank the leaders of the externally focused churches who have allowed us to share their stories in this book. If there ever comes a day that the term *externally focused church* is redundant, we will have these and many other churches to thank for leading the way.

—**Rick Rusaw and Eric Swanson**
June, 2004

"We make a living by what we get; we make a life by what we give."

—Winston Churchill

Introduction

A number of years ago, while speaking to a small group of pastors, Chuck Colson described a national prayer breakfast he had recently attended. Colson said that the room was full of powerful people. The president of the United States, congressmen, senators, leaders of industry, and heads of state were all in attendance. However, he noted that the most powerful person in the room had no title, was small in stature, and had few financial resources. But when she spoke, even presidents listened. Mother Teresa's power stemmed not from position, title, or wealth but from her role as servant. She had earned the right to be heard through a lifetime of service.

No one would argue that Christians shouldn't serve. Jesus said he had come to serve, not to be served. The early church served. Service is, and should be, the identifying mark of Christians and the church.

But every statistic tells us that the church in America today is becoming more and more marginalized and less and less influential. We don't need another Barna study to tell us that fewer people feel the church can help them. There are many reasons for this, but two stand out. First, as messengers, Christians have a difficult task, not because the message isn't compelling, but because we aren't always compelling messengers. In fact, we are often our own worst enemies. Society is no longer scandalized by improprieties among those who claim to follow Christ; it has come to expect them. Second, we have to tell the truth to a world that no longer believes in truth. John Bruce, pastor of Creekside Community Church in San Leandro, California, describes this dilemma. "For so many years I felt that my evangelism was like presenting my case before a jury, but the judge wouldn't allow me to present any evidence."[1]

One of the most effective ways to reach people with the message of Jesus Christ today is through real and relevant acts of service. Honest, compassionate service can restore credibility to the crucial message we have to share. To *tell* the truth, we must *show* the truth. It's the model Jesus used. He served. He met needs. People listened. Erwin McManus, pastor of Mosaic, a church in Los Angeles, stated this simple yet powerful truth about sharing the message of Christ today: "People have given up on the truth because they don't believe anyone can be trusted."[2] The world is full of people who have been hurt by those who were supposed to love them—people they should have been able to trust. Before churches will be heard, they must re-establish trust. To establish trust, they must first show their ability to love.

Two items clearly reveal the truth about what matters most to us: our checkbooks and our calendars. Regardless of what we claim, how we spend our money and our time exposes what truly matters to us. Likewise, if we were to examine church calendars and budgets, we could determine fairly quickly what really matters most to our churches today. Is it what mattered to Jesus?

Churches talk about service, and everyone agrees that it ought to be important to us, but do we really know how to effectively meet the needs of our communities and reach lost people? Are we willing to step outside the safety net of our church pews and cross the street into real-life, real-world acts of service in order to share the truth of Jesus Christ?

The Externally Focused Church

There is a movement creeping its way across churches of all shapes, sizes, and denominations. It's gaining ground, it's getting attention, and it's making a difference. It's slowly changing church statistics. These churches are evaluating what really matters, and they are reaching skeptical, hurt, and broken people through serving. How are these churches changing the relationship between the church and their communities? How are they getting a skeptical society to hear them? They are externally focused, and this is what defines them:

They are inwardly strong but outwardly focused.

They integrate good deeds and good news into the life of the church.

They value impact and influence in the community more than attendance.

They seek to be salt, light, and leaven in the community.

They see themselves as the "soul" of the community.

They would be greatly missed by the community if they left.

Remember Show and Tell in third grade? It seems as if the church has become more concerned with telling than showing. Christians will tell others what they need to do to be right with God, to be better people. Christians will proclaim what isn't right with the world. Christians know how to tell about God's love and why it is needed in people's lives. For the most part, though, our churches have forgotten to *show* God's love. And all too often, what we do show doesn't match up with what we tell.

Today, whether we like it or not, we have to earn the right to be heard. As we've all heard many times, "People don't care how much you know until they know how much you care." *Showing* through serving can help Christians and churches *tell* more effectively. The success of an externally focused church depends on getting involved in the community, creating authentic relationships, and being truly useful. In the process of showing, externally focused churches have discovered, again and again, that people are more willing to listen to their telling.

Who Is This Book For?

This book is written with two types of churches in mind. First is the *externally committed* church. These churches are already externally focused in what they do, but they want to learn what others are doing so they can excel even more. They want to increase the number of people deployed into the community where they can be salt, light, and leaven—agents of transformation. Or they may want to increase the frequency of service or the depth of that service—moving from service into *relationship*. They also want to learn how to leverage and increase their impact by beginning new ministries or partnering with existing efforts.

Second is the *externally curious* church. These churches have heard about this growing movement and want more information on how to become an externally focused church. They ask, "How did they do it?" and "How can we do it?" In both cases, by the end of the book we hope to have answered three questions:

- Why should we be an externally focused church?

- What are we trying to accomplish?

- How can we get started or improve on what we are doing?

The results of an externally focused ministry are not entirely predictable. It's certain that the church will get its feet wet and probably muddy. At the very least, it will have benefited the community through its service. By becoming externally focused, churches have the chance to build relational bridges, giving Christians opportunities to share God's grace in the midst of real need. In this way, the church can transform lives as people both see and hear God's grace at work in their world—a church that is showing *and* telling.

Endnotes

1. John Bruce, comments (San Leandro, CA: sermon at Creekside Community Church, May 11, 2003).

2. Erwin McManus, comments (San Diego, CA: National Outreach Convention, September 2003).

chapter one

What Is an **Externally Focused** Church?

"There is nothing more powerful than an idea whose time has come."

—Victor Hugo

Ignited

In the summer of 2002, a number of forest fires burned out of control in Colorado for days at a time. The fire nearest to our community was between Denver and Estes Park in the Arapahoe National Forest. Although the fire was over twenty miles away, the sky above us was a cinnamon color, and smoke filled the air. With so much acreage burning and so much property destroyed, most of us assumed that it was the most important fire at the time. By the end of 2002, satellites recorded over a million fires around the globe that year[1]—places of light and heat that, quite independently of one another, ignited because the conditions were right.

Few people observing a nearby fire realize that on the same day an average of over twenty-seven hundred fires are ablaze in the forests and grasslands elsewhere on earth. It is only from the perspective of space and time that patterns of such magnitude and significance can be seen. In the same way, pastors and Christian leaders all around the world are beginning to think differently

Goodness & good deeds

about church. Independently of one another, they are increasingly convinced that effectiveness is not measured by what happens inside the church but rather by the impact the people of the church have on their communities. They are engaging their communities with truth and grace, good news and good deeds. They are becoming the salt that preserves, the light that shines upon, and the leaven that transforms a community. But what they may not realize is that they are part of a growing global movement.

These are the externally focused churches. And we believe that the externally focused church is an idea whose time has come. One pastor expressed it this way: "Either God has caused this wave that we are riding, or we have formed a wave that God is blessing. In either case, the wave is here." Are you ready to catch this wave?

Defining an Externally Focused Church

As we begin the story, it's probably best to begin with some definitions. We don't know of any churches that claim to be internally focused, but they exist all the same. Internally focused churches concentrate on getting people into the church and generating activity there. These churches may create powerful worship experiences, excel in teaching, offer thriving youth programs, and have vibrant small groups, but at the end of the day, what is measured is the number of people and activities within the church. These are good churches filled with good people. And what they do is vital but not sufficient for a healthy church. Worship, teaching, and personal devotions are absolutely necessary for building the internal capacity necessary to sustain an external focus, but if all the human and financial resources are expended inside the four walls of the church, then no matter how "spiritual" things may appear to be, something is missing.

In many churches today, people are rediscovering the majesty of God and expressing their praise through worship. Music is no longer just the warm-up for the message. There is expectancy that God inhabits the praises of his people (from Psalm 22:3, King James Version). But worship that is not manifested in how we live in relationship with others may be hollow. We aren't the first ones to experience this. In the years preceding the Babylonian captivity, Isaiah had a message from God concerning Israel's "internal" focus—along with an exhortation to move beyond formal worship to true righteousness:

> Stop bringing meaningless offerings! Your incense is detestable to me...I cannot bear your evil assemblies...They have become a burden to me; I am weary of bearing them. When you spread out your hands in prayer, I will hide my eyes from you; even if you offer many prayers, I will not listen...Stop doing wrong, learn to do right! *Seek justice, encourage the oppressed. Defend the cause of the fatherless, plead the case of the widow* (from Isaiah 1:13-17, emphasis added).

Throughout this prophetic book, Isaiah exposes the inadequacy of the faith of people who focus on loving God but forget about loving man. Addressing the futility of prayers and fasting in the absence of concern for others, God says, "Is not this the kind of fasting I have chosen: to loose the chains of injustice and untie the cords of the yoke, to set the oppressed free and break every yoke? Is it not to share your food with the hungry and to provide the poor wanderer with shelter—when you see the naked, to clothe him?" (Isaiah 58:6-7a).

Externally focused churches are internally strong, but they are oriented externally. Their external focus is reflected in those things for which they staff and budget. Because they engage their communities with the good works and good news of Jesus Christ, their communities are better places in which to live. These churches look for ways to be useful to their communities, to be a part of their hopes and dreams. They build bridges to their communities instead of walls around themselves. They don't shout at the dirty stream; they get in the water and begin cleaning it up. They determine their effectiveness not only by internal measures—such as attendance, worship, teaching, and small groups—but also by external measures: the spiritual and societal effects they are having on the communities around them. Externally focused churches measure not only what can be counted but also what matters most—the impact they are having outside the four walls of the church. They ask, "Whose lives are different because of this church?" Nearly everything that is done inside the church should prepare and equip people not only for

Whose lives are different because of this church?

personal growth but also for personal impact. Like every church, externally focused churches have their problems and challenges, but they are determined to make a difference in society. Internally focused churches help individuals, but externally focused churches change the world. Could your church change the world?

Who Is the Target Audience?

Of course, we need to ask, "Who is the recipient of all of this externally focused energy?" Pete Menconi, of Greenwood Community Church near Denver, recently said that an externally focused church must be externally focused everywhere it ministers, "from Jerusalem to Judea and Samaria to the remotest part of the earth." And he's right. Greenwood has long been a leader in serving those outside the church through nearly fifty externally focused partner ministries. But this book is not about foreign missions per se (though it can and should have implications for church planters). This book addresses how a church relates to *the community in which it resides.*

Although everyone outside the church is a potential ministry focus, the externally focused church moves toward two specific groups. *The first group comprises those on the margins.* God has a special place in his heart for those on the margins of society—and a plan for his people to minister to these broken people. There are nearly four hundred biblical passages demonstrating God's concern for orphans, widows, prisoners, aliens, the homeless, the poor, the hungry, the sick, and the disabled. "[God] defends the cause of the fatherless and the widow, and loves the alien, giving him food and clothing. And you are to love those who are aliens, for you yourselves were aliens in Egypt" (Deuteronomy 10:18-19).

God also made provisions in the law for his people to use special offerings to look out for those living on the edge. "At the end of every three years, bring all the tithes of that year's produce and store it in your towns, so that the Levites (who have no allotment or inheritance of their own) and the aliens, the fatherless and the widows who live in your towns may come and eat and be satisfied" (Deuteronomy 14:28-29a). He commanded the farmers and vintners to not squeeze every bit of profit out of the land but always to leave some behind for the poor to harvest (Deuteronomy 24:19-22). And God asks us to open our hearts and be generous. "Give generously to him and do so without a grudging heart; then because of this the Lord your God will bless you in all your work and in everything you put your hand to. There will always be poor people in the land. Therefore I command you to be openhanded toward your brothers and toward the poor and needy in your land" (Deuteronomy 15:10-11). God cares for everyone who is made in his image, and he wants his church to do the same.

Micheal Elliott, president of Union Mission in Savannah, Georgia, makes the point that the homeless, the incarcerated, widows, orphans, and immigrants generally lack a social support system. As the largest social support system in the United States, the church has the potential to greatly expand the kingdom by providing social support for those who have none.[2]

Glen Kehrein is the founding director of Circle Urban Ministries in Chicago. For over twenty-five years, he and his family have been making a difference among the poor and needy in Chicago. He knows the joys and heartaches of ministering to those on the fringes. One evening over dinner, Glen told about going to hear a well-known authority present a seminar titled "Eight Characteristics of Healthy Churches." The characteristics included evangelistic vitality, small groups, and dynamic worship. He returned from the seminar shaking his head, astonished that no mention was made of ministering to those on the margins whom God cares so much about. "How can you have a healthy church that has no concern for the poor?" Churches that are externally focused come alongside those in society who are under-resourced and disenfranchised.

John Perkins, the recognized founder of the Christian Community Development Association (CCDA), a national organization of urban ministers, says, "Not everyone is called to move to the inner-city to minister there, but everyone is called to have a heart for hurting people."[3] Are there people in your community who need an extra dose of mercy? Are there any hurting, broken people who long to be noticed and cared for? Erwin McManus, pastor of Mosaic in Los Angeles, says that the church "offers community to those who have no community."[4] The Scriptures say, "God sets the lonely in families" (Psalm 68:6). Are you willing to offer community to those who have no community? Are you willing to be family to those who have no families?

The second recipient of the externally focused church's energy is the city. Externally focused churches have moved past being angry with the city to wanting to be a blessing to the city. Much has been written about "taking back our cities" for God, but really, much of this is testosterone-driven language that reinforces the idea of being at war with the city.

This is not the language of Jesus. Probably the verse most of us remember from Jeremiah 29 is verse 11: " 'For I know the plans I have for you,' declares the Lord, 'plans to prosper you and not to harm you, plans to give you hope and a future.' " This is the kind of verse everyone likes to hear. But have you ever gone back to the beginning of the passage? It's really a message from God to those "Nebuchadnezzar had carried into exile from Jerusalem to Babylon" (Jeremiah 29:1). The Israelites were now captive people living in foreign lands in what is now Iraq. God advises them how to live as strangers and aliens. He tells them to join in the life and rhythms of the city: "Build houses and settle down; plant gardens and eat what they produce. Marry and have sons and daughters; find wives for your sons and give your daughters in marriage, so that they too may have sons and daughters. Increase in number there; do not decrease" (Jeremiah 29:4-6).

The key verse in this message pertains to their relationship with the city: "Also, seek the peace and prosperity of the city to which I have carried you into exile. Pray to the Lord for it because if it prospers, you too will prosper" (verse 7, emphasis added). What? Pray for this godless, pagan city? You've got to be kidding! Nope. That's what God said. So the believers were to do two things: actively seek the peace and prosperity of the city and pray for the city. (By the way, this is how both Daniel and Nehemiah gained such favor with the city's inhabitants.) Externally focused churches look for ways to seek and promote the welfare of the city.

Most school districts face tough times. In 2001 Kansas City was hit by economic hardships and the accompanying sagging morale of teachers and administrators. The previous twenty years had seen eighteen superintendents come and seventeen of them leave. Rather than wringing his hands, Pastor Adam Hamilton of United Methodist Church of the Resurrection in Leawood, Kansas, decided to do something to bless his city. From the pulpit, he challenged teachers and administrators in his suburban congregation to *now!!*

leave their suburban jobs and begin teaching in the inner city. He also had cards available, addressed to every employee of the Kansas City School District—all 5,700 of them. He challenged each person in attendance (approximately 5,700 people) to take a card, to pray for the person named on it, and, as God would lead, to write a note of encouragement and thanks to that teacher, administrator, custodian, or cafeteria worker. The cards weren't bulk-mailed from the church; rather, each person addressed and stamped a personal letter and included a personal return address on the envelope. Many included their phone numbers and offers to help.

The response of the teachers and staff was tremendous. They were overwhelmed by the encouragement and offers of support. Many contacted the individuals, and as a result, many members of the Church of the Resurrection are now involved in tutoring and reading programs in inner-city schools. Church of the Resurrection figured out a simple way to be a blessing to its community. This stuff is not rocket science. Any church of any size can be a blessing.

A Beautiful Thing

Do you remember Jesus' first miracle? He didn't raise someone from the dead. He didn't feed the multitudes or heal someone of a debilitating illness. He turned the water in six stone jars into fine wine at a wedding—simply because the host had run out of wine. Jesus "revealed his glory" by seeking the welfare of the host and guests of the wedding in Cana. His presence was a blessing to the wedding. Everyone was glad that Jesus showed up, but his act also led to spiritual transformation, as "his disciples put their faith in him" (John 2:11).

A young man walks toward a woman whose age is belied by the joy and sparkle in her eyes. The man extends his hand and asks the seated woman, "May I have this dance?" And so begins the Mariners' Senior Prom—an evening of dancing, food, and fun sponsored by the Lighthouse Ministry of Mariners Church in Irvine, California, for seniors from a convalescent home in the community. Young men dance with elderly women, and young women take the arms of older gentlemen. Walkers and canes are put away for the evening. For tonight is a night to dance—to feel the joy of youth, to hear music from days gone by.

Two hundred men and a smattering of women and children gather around elevated television screens scattered throughout a room. It's Super Bowl Sunday. Tables and chairs are arranged for optimum viewing and optimum interaction, but men still jockey for the seats closest to the TV sets. On the tables are hot chicken wings, five-layer bean dip, meatballs, nachos, chips, guacamole, pizza—snacks befitting a world championship event. In the finest room Lake Avenue Church has to offer, the homeless have gathered for a Sunday afternoon in Pasadena. These are men whose candle is nearly extinguished. To be cheering for their team, to feel some sort of passion, reassures them that they are still alive. And for an afternoon at least, a community is created for those who have no community.

A dance and a Super Bowl party...what do they mean? Are they expressions of mercy? Are they expressions of justice? Maybe they simply reflect love—doing unto a neighbor what you'd like done for you if you were in his or her shoes. When a woman poured out a flask of perfume on Jesus, the disciples exclaimed indignantly, "Why this waste?...This perfume could have been sold at a high price and the money given to the poor" (Matthew 26:8-9). The spiritual bookkeepers of the world love a return on their investments, but what Jesus asks us to do can't be measured in those terms. Jesus replied to the disciples, "She has done a beautiful thing to me" (Matthew 26:10b). Sometimes things shouldn't be measured in terms of better and best, but of beauty.

Externally focused churches bring beauty to their communities. Their love is a garland of grace. They don't just hand out soup; sometimes they serve nachos. They don't just hand out winter coats; sometimes they help pick out a prom dress.

To be a blessing to their cities, externally focused churches go way beyond traditional methodologies. Through arts, drama, and sports, they create opportunities to influence the lives of children and youth. By offering classes to the community in public settings such as banks, hospitals, and hotel conference rooms, they equip emerging workforces with skills necessary to thrive.

Externally Focused Churches Are Not Limited by Size, Location, or Denomination

Size has nothing to do with a church's ability to be externally focused. The operative word is *focus*. Remember Jesus' words, "For where two or three come together in my name, there am I with them" (Matthew 18:20). Several years ago Scott Beck, the first franchisee and eventual chief operating officer of Blockbuster Video, was addressing a group of ministry leaders. The discussion centered on the meaning of *critical mass*. Scott was asked, "What does it take to launch a venture…to get it off the ground?" Scott's answer was concise: "*Critical mass is one person with a vision*."[5] Most likely, for your church to become externally focused, it will take one person with a vision. Perhaps that person is you!

Critical mass is one person with a vision.

Being externally focused has much more to do with mind-set than with size. In response to a request to relate the impact his church is having on its community, a pastor from a small town in central Florida excitedly talked about the church's work with recovering drug addicts. To provide work for these folks, the church started a construction business and an auto-repair shop. It obtained a contract to turn military Humvees into civilian vehicles. Every week members of the church also minister to prisoners in the local jail. One would think this man pastors a church of a thousand or more, but in reality it is a church of around 250! The church's membership is modest, but its impact is huge.

Location is not part of what it means to be externally focused. Although we often associate ministering to the needs of the community exclusively with the urban church, externally focused churches may be found in urban, rural, and suburban settings.[6] This book is not written exclusively, or even primarily, for urban churches. Of the 340,000 churches in North America, tens of thousands are not located in an urban setting. To all of these churches we say, "Come, join us on the journey."

Externally focused churches are not determined by denomination or style. No single denomination has the inside track on external impact.

Good Deeds/good News

"Seeker-sensitive churches," "purpose-driven churches," "megachurches," "equipping churches," "multiethnic churches," "house churches," "connected churches," and "multi-site churches" can all maintain their distinctive characteristics and still be externally focused. To be externally focused probably means returning to the reason your church was founded in the first place. Being externally focused cuts across all denominational and racial lines. Being externally focused is about *the perspective and purpose of the church* more than any program the church might engage in. Once a church decides to become externally focused by joining in the life and conversation of the community, the possibilities of *how* it engages the community are endless.

Four Characteristics of Externally Focused Churches

➤ **Externally focused churches are convinced that good deeds and good news can't and shouldn't be separated.** Just as it takes two wings to lift an airplane off the ground, so externally focused churches couple good news with good deeds to make an impact on their communities. The good deeds, expressed in service and ministry to others, validate the good news. The good news explains the purpose of the good deeds.

Good news and good deeds are, after all, the summation of Jesus' ministry. God proclaimed the *"good news...through Jesus Christ...and...he went around *doing good*...because God was with him"* (Acts 10:36-38, emphasis added). When the crowds were following Jesus, he "welcomed them and spoke to them about the kingdom of God [good news], and healed those who needed healing [good deeds]" (Luke 9:11). When Jesus sent the twelve disciples out, "he sent them out to preach the kingdom of God [good news] and to heal the sick [good deeds]" (Luke 9:2).

Engaging the community with good news and good deeds is not just a tactic or even a foundational strategy of externally focused churches; it is at their very core; it is who they are. These churches have concluded that it's really not "church" if it's not engaged in the life of the community through ministry and service to others. Ministry and service are not programs reserved for a few extraordinarily dedicated individuals but are woven into every aspect of church life. This is certainly not the only thing these churches do, but to stop ministering to and serving in the community would be to end their very existence. An external focus is embedded in their DNA.

Second, they see themselves as vital to the health and well-being of their communities. They believe that their communities, with all of their aspirations and challenges, cannot be truly healthy without the church's involvement. They have moved beyond thinking about the church's health apart from the community...to what the community would be like apart from the church. They recognize that God has placed them in their communities (whether they feel wanted or not) to be salt, light, and leaven. They are not social workers but kingdom builders!

They are not social workers but kingdom builders!

Why have so many churches emotionally or physically withdrawn from their communities? Sometimes churches feel unwanted. Whereas the church may once have been the center of the community, the community has changed its focus and left the church behind. Maybe this separation has something to do with the New Testament word for *church.* It is the word *ecclesia,* meaning "the called out ones." Many have mistaken this to mean a physical separation from the world. The church is called to be separate in lifestyle but never to be isolated from the people it seeks to influence. Salt, light, and leaven don't work very well from a distance.

Pastor Keith Zafren of River Church Community in San Jose, California, posits another idea. He notes that the theme of John Bunyan's *Pilgrim's Progress,* written in 1675, involves escaping the wicked city in pursuit of the celestial city. Keith points out that this theme of escaping the city has subconsciously influenced the church for over three hundred years! Could it also be that Christians have tried to turn the church into a celestial city where we can educate our kids, eat our meals after church, and enjoy our circle of friends away from the wicked city?[7]

yes!

It is only when the church is mixed into the very life and conversation of the city that it can be an effective force for change. In approximately A.D. 150, a Christian writer described the lifestyle of second-century Christians. Summing up his thoughts, he wrote, "As the soul is to the body, so Christians [are] to the *agents of influence not control!*

world."[8] Christians are nothing less than the very soul of the community. What happens when the soul is removed from the body? Nothing remains but a corpse or a shell. Externally focused churches recognize that the gospel is most powerful when Christians are living in face-to-face relationships with those in their communities. Addressing Christians' involvement in the community, the Christian writer Tertullian wrote:

> [Do we not] dwell beside you, sharing your way of life, your dress, your habits and the same needs of life? We are no Brahmins or Indian gymnosophists, dwelling in woods and exiled from life…We stay beside you in this world, making use of the forum, the provision-market, the bath, the booth, the workshop, the inn, the weekly market, and all other places of commerce. We sail with you, fight at your side, till the soil with you, and traffic with you; we likewise join our technical skill to that of others, and make our works public property for your use. [9]

Wow! The early Christians were not a society of separatists. They engaged in the life of the city. They socialized with their neighbors. They looked out for them. What about your church? Is it part of the warp and woof of the community?

In joining in the life and rhythm of the city, externally focused churches seek to serve and bless the city, not to control it. After all, salt, light, and leaven are agents of influence, not of control. Thus these churches build bridges instead of walls. They bless their cities and pray for them. They are one of the defined assets of their communities, not one of the liabilities.

Third, they believe that ministering and serving are the normal expressions of Christian living. Even more, they believe that Christians grow best when they are serving and giving themselves away to others. Because service and ministry are part of their growth model for the church and the spiritual formation of its people, it is not unusual for huge percentages of their congregations to serve and minister outside the walls of the church. Wanting to be like Jesus, who came not to be served but to serve and to give (Mark 10:45), externally focused churches serve and give themselves to

> **Christians can learn through good instruction, but they really cannot grow if they remain uninvolved in ministry and service.**

others. They are convinced that Christians can learn through good instruction, but they really cannot grow if they remain uninvolved in ministry and service.

Fourth, externally focused churches are evangelistically effective. It's no secret that the church in North America is not hitting the ball out of the park evangelistically. Church attendance has dropped from a high of 49 percent in 1991 to 43 percent in 2002.[10] While the U.S. population grew by 9 percent between 1992 and 1999, the median adult attendance per church service has dropped 12 percent during the same time frame.[11] A study initiated by Hartford Seminary and conducted by Faith Communities Today (FACT) of more than 14,000 congregations showed that only half of the congregations are growing.[12] Much perceived growth is simply transfer growth between churches. Attendance at two-thirds of U.S. churches has either plateaued or is declining. According to a study by the American Religious Identification Survey (ARIS) of over 50,000 American households in 2001, "the proportion of the population that can be classified as Christian has declined from 86 percent in 1990 to 77 percent in 2001."[13] It's a sad day when at the annual meeting, the chairman of the board reports, "We didn't have any conversions this year, giving is down, and we're $20,000 in debt, but praise God, no other churches in our town are doing better."

The good news for externally focused churches, according to the FACT study, is "congregations with a strong commitment to social justice and with direct participation in community outreach ministries are more likely to be growing than other congregations."[14]

The demographics of our country are changing. Fewer people claim a Christian heritage. Recently at Rocky Mountain Christian Church in Longmont, Colorado, a man in his thirties shared his conversion testimony with the congregation. He was an auto mechanic who had never darkened the door of a church. He had never been to a Christian wedding or funeral. He had never attended an Easter or Christmas service. He asked a friend to take him to church because he "didn't know how to go to church."

What? He didn't know how to go to church? Who wouldn't know how to go to church? But think of it this way…would you know how to go to a Buddhist temple? How about a mosque? Do you know if these institutions have open seating or assigned seats? Do they expect nonbelievers to follow the same external patterns of bowing or kneeling as the true believers? There's a lot to know.

We must accept the fact that an increasingly large portion of our population has no idea of "how to go to church." Externally focused churches have the advantage of deploying people into the community where they can *be* church to people through their love and service. Their light is not hidden under a bushel. No, they are letting their light shine. You'll learn about these churches in this book.

Although these churches serve their communities expecting nothing in return, many people are drawn into the kingdom through their presence, service, and love. The Bible tells us that Peter encountered a "paralytic who had been bedridden for eight years. 'Aeneas,' Peter said to him, 'Jesus Christ heals you. Get up...' Immediately Aeneas got up. All those who lived in Lydda and Sharon saw him and turned to the Lord" (Acts 9:33-35). It could be argued that these folks turned to the Lord because their friend was healed. But the healed man was simply the evidence of the existence, love, and power of the healer, Jesus. After observing Jesus' compassion and love, people responded, "God has come to help his people" (Luke 7:16b).

In our evangelistic zeal, we often think people just need more or better information in order to believe. But what they really long for is authenticity. Fewer are asking, "What must I do to be saved?" Instead their question is "What can I do to make my life work?" When the people who talk about a loving God demonstrate love, the gap between doubt and faith is narrowed, and the people around them often find themselves wanting to believe.

Leesburg, Florida, a town of about twenty thousand people, is just a speck on the map of central Florida, yet it has one of the best examples we've seen of an externally focused church. First Baptist Church has spawned nearly seventy ministries to intersect the physical, emotional, and spiritual needs of the people in Leesburg. Through their Men's Shelter, Women's Care Center, Latchkey Ministry, Children's Home, Benevolence Ministry, and other ministries, they regularly lead hundreds of people to Christ and disciple them in maturity and service. Senior Pastor Charles Roesel says, "The only way the gospel can be biblically shared is to focus on the whole person, with all [his or her] hurts and needs, and to involve the church in ministering to those persons and leading them to Christ. This is the essence of our ministry evangelism."[15]

Vineyard Community Church of Cincinnati, through its servant evangelism ("showing others the love of Christ with no strings attached") regularly sees hundreds of people come to faith each year. This is founding pastor Steve Sjogren's admonition to church planters: "Don't go to start a church...go to serve a city. Serve them with love, and if you go after the people nobody wants, you'll end up with the people everybody

---
Don't go to start a church...go to serve a city.

---

wants."[16] Each Saturday you will find this church engaged in practical ways to show the love of Christ to Cincinnati. Its members might be washing cars or handing out bottled water or delivering groceries to hungry families. People are drawn to such places of light. People are looking for places of authenticity where the walk matches the talk—where faith is making a difference. These words are carved in stone over the entrance of the church: "Small things done with great love will change the world." Vineyard *is* changing the world.

Two Strategies of Externally Focused Churches

First, a few comments about "models." Models represent a simplified view of reality. Different models give us different options. Models can represent "what is" or "what could be." The point we want to make about models is that there are a number of effective ways to engage your community with good news and good deeds. We will present a lot of models, but there is no "right" model. A good model is one that accomplishes the desired outcomes and is consistent with the heart and desires of our Lord. So look for principles within the models that you can apply.

Churches that are externally focused usually have variations of two strategies at their disposal. *First, they identify needs of their communities and start ministries or programs to meet those needs.* For example, they may start food banks, learning centers, or English as a Second Language (ESL) programs for immigrants. Experienced churches often form separate nonprofit spin-offs under which a ministry can be organized. This separate 501(c)(3) status often allows them to receive outside corporate and government funding to get the resources required by large-scale endeavors such as affordable housing, food banks, and homes for unwed mothers.

Second, they partner with existing ministries or human-service agencies that are already accomplishing a shared mission in the community. Nearly every community has a number of human-service agencies that are morally positive and spiritually neutral and are doing their best to meet the needs of the under-served and under-resourced people of the community. Such agencies include the food bank, homeless shelter, emergency family housing, and safe house for abused women.

In addition, externally focused churches recognize that other church or parachurch ministries are effective in ministering to specific target audiences (such as youth, unwed mothers, and the unemployed). Rather than starting a new ministry, these human-service agencies and church or parachurch organizations can serve as "partner ministries" of a local congregation. Churches can simply join what is already happening in the community. Instead of each congregation having its own food pantry, why not partner with the local food bank? When hungry people request food, congregations refer these folks to their partner ministries. Likewise, when people come to the community food bank with more than a physical hunger, they are referred to one of the churches.

It Wasn't About the Donkey

Riding a donkey, Jesus entered Jerusalem on Palm Sunday. The crowds cheered and shouted praises to him. They lopped off palm fronds and laid them on the ground for the donkey to walk on. When they ran out of palm branches, they gladly laid their own cloaks on the ground and, walking ahead of Jesus and the donkey, shouted, "Hosanna to the Son of David! Blessed is he who comes in the name of the Lord. Hosanna in the highest!" (Matthew 21:9). For a moment the donkey perhaps thought it was all about him. After all, he was doing all the work that morning. But it wasn't about him. It had nothing to do with him. He was simply carrying the Message.

The externally focused church is a good donkey that takes Jesus into places where he hasn't always been welcome. The serving church is just the donkey. It's still all about Jesus. We're glad you are joining us on this journey. The fire that is spreading is a good fire. Lives will be saved, not harmed. It's going to be a great ride.

Something to **Think** About

"Externally focused churches measure not only what can be counted but also what matters most." After reading this chapter, what do you think matters to God in this world? What really matters to you?

Something to **Talk** About

1. When was the last time you were really proud of what your church was doing?

2. Is your church an internally focused church or an externally focused church? How can you tell?

3. Can you imagine how different your community would be if every follower of Christ in every church in your community began loving and serving others in a meaningful way?

4. What do you think would happen in the lives of the followers?

5. What do you think would happen in the churches?

6. What do you think would happen to the community?

Something to **Act** Upon

1. If "*critical mass* is one person with a vision," is it possible that you are that person? Why or why not?

2. After reading this chapter, what possibilities come to mind about what your church could become?

3. Who could you talk to about joining you in exploring new possibilities?

Sermon/**Lesson** Idea

Text: Isaiah 58:1-12

Main Idea: Isaiah 58 addresses two types of people and two types of churches: those that are internally focused, as illustrated by fasting and seeking God but doing nothing about the needs around them, and those that are externally focused, as demonstrated by their giving themselves in service to others.

Illustration: Jesus' ministry of good news and good deeds (Acts 10:36-38)

Action Point: Will you accept the challenge to become an externally focused church?

Endnotes

1. Ivan Csiszar, Ph.D, written comments (University of Maryland, February 5, 2004).
2. Micheal Elliott, comments (Savannah, GA: conversation with Eric Swanson at Union Mission, February 3, 2004).
3. John Perkins, comments (Pasadena, CA: CCDA conference, Lake Avenue Community Church, November 2002).
4. Erwin Raphael McManus, comments (Los Angeles, CA: conversation at Mosaic with Eric Swanson, May 22, 2002).
5. Scott Beck, comments (Fort Collins, CO: meeting attended by regional directors of Campus Crusade for Christ and Eric Swanson, Colorado State University, June 28, 1995).
6. There are many fine books that focus on the needs of burgeoning cities and the role the church can play in ministering to them. In the list of resources (see page 224), we have included several good books written by the leaders and practitioners of urban ministry that may be helpful to people faced with the specific challenges of urban locations.

   It is interesting to note that for African-American churches, an external focus is not new. They have never differentiated between effective evangelism and efforts to meet the needs of those around them. A study of 2,150 black churches by C. Eric Lincoln and Lawrence H. Mamiya described in their book *The Black Church in the African American Experience* reports that nearly 70 percent of the total sample of black churches are involved with social [service] agencies or other nonchurch programs in dealing with community problems. New York City churches such as Concord Baptist Church of

Christ, Allen AME, Abyssinian Baptist, and Bethel Gospel Assembly, and Los Angeles churches such as First AME, Faithful Central Bible Church, and West Angeles COGIC, have led the way in transforming and preserving their communities.

7. Keith Zafren, comments (San Jose, CA: in a sermon titled "A Church in the City for the City," River Church Community, May 5, 2002).

8. Epistle of Mathetus to Diognetus, chapter 6, verse 25, www.ccel.org/fathers2/ANF-01/anf01-08.htm#P679_123511

9. Tertullian, as quoted in *The Expansion of Christianity in the First Three Centuries, vol. 1,* by Adolf Harnack (Eugene, OR: Wipf and Stock Publishers, 1998), 216.

10. Barna research online: www.barna.org/cgi-bin\PageCategory.asp?CategoryID=10

11. Barna Research Group, results of telephone poll.

12. Hartford, CT: Hartford Seminary/Faith Communities Today (FACT) study: www.fact.hart-sem.edu/executive_summary.htm

13. American Religious Identification Survey (ARIS), 2001.

14. Hartford, CT: FACT study.

15. Charles Roesel, comments (Leesburg, FL: conversation with Eric Swanson at First Baptist Church, April 8, 2003).

16. Steve Sjogren, comments (Cincinnati, OH: conversation with Eric Swanson, Vineyard Community Church, May 6, 2003).

chapter two

Becoming **Externally Focused**—
One Church's Journey

"One of the greatest pains to human nature is the pain of a new idea.
It...makes you think that after all, your favorite notions may be wrong, your
firmest beliefs ill-founded...Naturally, therefore, common men hate a new idea,
and are disposed more or less to ill-treat the original man who brings it."

—Walter Bagehot [1]

Focus

*The Hubble space telescope was launched from the space shuttle Discovery
on April 24, 1990. Expectations were high from the beginning, as
astronomers anticipated new discoveries and verification of their hypotheses
and theories. At launch time the Hubble project had cost over $1.5 billion to
create what would be the world's most powerful and accurate telescope. The
primary mirror, nearly eight feet across and weighing nearly a ton, was
ground as close to perfection as humanly possible. The curve did not deviate
by more than 1/800,000th of an inch. According to Hubble officials, if this
mirror "were scaled to the diameter of the Earth, the biggest bump would be
only six inches tall." Perched 353 miles above the Earth, the Hubble had an
unobstructed view and could peer light years into space to observe previously
undiscovered galaxies. But there was a problem. Soon after the Hubble was
set in orbit, engineers discovered that the main mirror was flawed. Objects*

that were supposed to be clear were fuzzy. The problem was not power or size. The problem was focus. The Hubble had to be repaired. So in December 1993, astronauts aboard the space shuttle Endeavor fitted the mirror with corrective optics. The mission was a complete success. The repairs corrected Hubble's previously blurry vision and allowed the telescope to explore the universe with unprecedented precision and clarity.[2] Only when the Hubble was focused, could it carry out the mission for which it was created. Size is important. Power is important. But focus is everything.

Few churches would say they are not interested in making a difference in their communities. Dr. Joe Ellis called the church "God's enterprise" in the world—God's business.[3] Unfortunately, many churches in America have lost their market share and failed to produce a profit and should be displaying a "going out of business" sign. If the church is God's enterprise, then Christians are entrepreneurs in that enterprise. Dictionaries define *entrepreneur* as one who is willing to assume the management and take the risk for the sake of profit. Jesus said if a tree doesn't bear fruit, tear it out and replace it with one that will. "Every tree that does not bear good fruit is cut down and thrown into the fire. Thus, by their fruit you will recognize them" (Matthew 7:19-20).

Jesus defined the kind of fruit he was looking for in the Great Commission: "Therefore go and make disciples of all nations, baptizing them in the name of the Father and of the Son and of the Holy Spirit, and teaching them to obey everything I have commanded you" (Matthew 28:19-20a).

Christians should be looking for exciting, authentic ways to produce fruit for the kingdom. Howard Hendricks of Dallas Theological Seminary once said, "I've never met a Christian who planned to live a mediocre life, but I have met plenty of mediocre Christians."[4] The same could be said of churches. One church, LifeBridge Christian Church in Longmont, Colorado, didn't want to drift toward mediocrity. This church has learned that service is a wonderful entry point for gaining a hearing in the community and for bearing fruit there. Here is the story, told by Rick, LifeBridge's senior minister.

Our Journey

What moves a church forward,

LifeBridge Christian Church is a vibrant congregation that was started over a hundred years ago. Our mission statement is "leading people in a growing relationship with Jesus Christ." LifeBridge has seen consistent growth over the years, and the church's leadership has always recognized the value of outreach. Though rich in heritage and tradition, our church is focused on being relevant and real in communicating the message of Christ to modern society. We've

> **We had always said we valued being a part of the community, but when we scrutinized how we deployed our resources, we realized that community involvement hadn't been a priority.**

always wanted to be a church that produces fruit; we've always wanted to be good stewards of God's enterprise. By all appearances, it seemed that we were doing these things. Several years ago, however, our church's leadership began a careful evaluation of all our efforts.

Like all churches, we were engaged in a number of ministries. (There is no end to ideas for activities the church can be involved in!) As we evaluated each one, we discovered that in some cases, activities that once may have seemed essential to our ministry were no longer useful or needed. In each case, we had to decide what truly moved the church closer to achieving its mission.

We had always said we valued being a part of the community, but when we scrutinized how we deployed our resources, we realized that community involvement hadn't been a priority. We had a benevolence ministry, but no intentional strategy for the people of LifeBridge to get involved in it. Several years ago, a member of one community-service agency told us, "The people of LifeBridge can be counted on to provide lots of gifts and even dollars, but they don't show up and get their hands dirty." It was hard to hear, but it was an accurate indictment. When we studied how we spent our treasure, we realized she was right. Our greatest resource—people—was underutilized and we were missing out on the blessing of serving people outside the church. In addition, we weren't finding effective ways to create relationships outside of our four walls.

We realized that we often felt we'd done our part by donating money or other material goods to worthy causes. While these things are certainly needed, donating them doesn't require any actual involvement and often serves only to relieve guilt. Jesus didn't wait for one of the household servants to wash the feet of the disciples; he took a towel and basin, knelt, and got his hands dirty. We recognized that there will always be a need for money and other goods, but giving them should never be at the expense of actually doing the work.

> **If our goal is to teach the truth to our children, it's likely to be our "modeling" and not our "mouthing" that gets the job done.**

We began to change the way we do ministry, and as a result, we began to change the image of our church in the community. As we tried to become more externally focused, we began to see that it wasn't about adding one more ministry to the thirty or so we already had; it was about a churchwide effort to focus on others, not ourselves. After pursuing this vision for several years, we are seeing lives changed, people connecting with God, and a growing spiritual maturity among our church family that is unprecedented in our church's history.

The changes we made to be an externally focused church did not happen overnight, and they did not happen by accident. Six key decisions laid the groundwork for all that followed. Here's what we decided to do:

1. We decided to broaden our outreach focus.

LifeBridge has always had a mission of reaching lost people. Through the years, the church has adapted and changed locations, methods, and worship styles in order to be culturally relevant. We understand and embrace the responsibility to take "the gospel that never changes to a world that will never be the same." Outreach is very important to the church's leaders, staff, and members. In the 1990s the main strategy for outreach at LifeBridge was creating large special events, especially surrounding Christmas and Easter, to attract visitors. A lot of time and money were poured into these special events, and thousands of people visited the church because of them. They were intended to introduce people to LifeBridge in the hope that they would return for worship. That strategy did lead to the church's growth, and it was a first step for many families who are now an active part of our church.

Our "Dickens Christmas" was very successful in nearly every way. More than a thousand people in the church volunteered their time and talents to produce it. It was a unique Christmas event involving live carolers, street performers, school choirs, community groups, drama troupes, craft rooms, story rooms, a dinner theater, and a Nativity drama. Members of the entire community and beyond made it a part of their annual Christmas activities. Many of our new members first encountered LifeBridge through this event. The last year we held the event, it attracted thirty-two thousand people! It attracted plenty of media coverage. In every way we could measure, it was successful.

But, for a number of reasons, we decided to make a change. We had a change in the ministry staff that led the event, it took a lot of money to produce, it required a great deal of our staff resources, and ultimately, it was internally focused. Although it was an event for the community, it asked the community to come to us. Although it had been successful for a long time, it was clear that our image in the community was mostly tied to "Dickens Christmas" and other special events. To redirect our focus more intentionally outward meant a change. It meant looking for new ways to get to know our community and be of service.

For a number of years, we had been getting more and more involved in the community through service. In the public schools, police department, and other community organizations, we had been finding ways to help meet a variety of needs in our community. We realized that one of the most effective ways to communicate the shift in thinking to our congregation was by changing our focus during the Christmas season. Instead of producing a large-scale event geared toward bringing the community to us, we created short-term service opportunities that would allow the people of LifeBridge to go out into the community. We told them, "For the last several years we have worked hard to invite people to come here. This year we want to expend the same kind of energy in the community." And that is how A Time to Serve was born (see "A Closer Look" on page 40).

While it is still a special event, it is focused externally, on meeting the needs of our community at Christmas. A Time to Serve is a several-week, churchwide opportunity to serve. Were the people of LifeBridge interested? A resounding "yes" came from people of all ages in the church. People said, "This is the best thing our church has ever done." It has opened doors for people in the church to find ways of serving in the community throughout the year.

Big events are still a part of outreach at LifeBridge, but they are no longer the main focus. We balance outreach events with ongoing engagement with the community through serving. We channel our church members into the community to serve, not just encourage them to participate in church-led activities at the church facility. Church members are stepping up to the challenge of living out their faith through serving.

A Closer Look

A Time to Serve

LifeBridge Christian Church encourages everyone in the church to participate in serving the community from Thanksgiving through Christmas. These weeks of service are entry-level ways of preparing and equipping LifeBridge people to be externally focused. During this Time to Serve, we partner with other community organizations to perform needed services. Preparation begins as early as September as LifeBridge staff and volunteer coordinators contact local agencies to determine the community's needs. In November the sign-ups begin! During every weekend in November, we print detailed information about the opportunities to serve. Church members and attenders choose from more than thirty projects. Here are just a few of the service projects:

- painting and cleaning at a transitional housing facility
- winterizing mobile homes at a local senior citizen trailer park
- distributing Christmas gifts with the community assistance program
- assembling and distributing holiday food baskets
- renovating a new community childcare center for low-income families
- free gift-wrapping at the local Kmart
- working with the public schools' evening maintenance crews
- cleaning and painting the local humane society
- serving with the Division of Wildlife in park restoration and cleanup

- working with the county to clear trees to create a fire line
- maintaining and painting a local crisis pregnancy center

More than fifteen hundred adults and children (almost half of our church) give more than six thousand hours in community service during this period. It is the first opportunity for many people to be involved in the church beyond coming to worship. And many bring their friends and family members to serve with them.

Karen's husband rarely comes to church with her, but when she told him about the opportunity to volunteer as a family with the County Parks and Open Space, he was happy to give it a try. During their hours volunteering, clearing trees, and cleaning up trash, this man met a minister at our church and learned they had a lot in common. When the second Time to Serve came around, the husband didn't wait for his wife to ask if he wanted to serve. He saw a church bulletin insert, circled the service opportunities he was interested in, and excitedly told her, "Sign me up!" This husband, who previously had no interest in going to church, is slowly building a sense of community with Christians through serving—and has been in church a little more this year than last.

2. We decided not to create something that already exists.

Traditionally, when Christians haven't liked what's going on in schools, they've started their own schools. If they didn't like what was happening in some business organizations, they began their own. When they didn't like secular music, they created their own industry. As a result, we now have "Christian" versions of nearly everything. Instead of influencing the cultural stream, we've created our own parallel stream. At LifeBridge, we decided to come alongside schools, service organizations, and other nonprofits (religious and secular) to see how we could help them. These partnerships have enabled us to be good stewards of our resources and of theirs. Instead of starting our own food program, we asked members to contribute volunteer time as well as food and other resources to the local food bank. Instead of doing our own angel tree Christmas *engaged in the public school.*

project, we participate in the community-led project by asking volunteers to sort, package, and deliver gifts. Instead of creating our own Christian school, we are purposefully engaged in the public schools. Instead of creating our own processes and programs, LifeBridge has made a concerted effort to partner with those organizations and community leaders who are already trying to meet needs. In doing so, we have benefited from amicable relationships with these organizations instead of competitive ones.

What about good news?

A Closer Look

Should We Start a Christian School?

Like many churches, LifeBridge was being pressed fairly hard to begin a Christian school. We really wrestled with the idea and saw plenty of benefits for church members and the community if we were to do so. We asked ourselves some basic questions.

Why would we want a school? The overwhelming answer was "to be able to provide a faith-based education that will positively influence students."

If we had our own school, how many students could we affect? A quick calculation of the community's student population revealed that at the time, we would have been able to connect with less than 2.5 percent of the student population.

Who has significant influence over the lives of students? Peers, parents, and other influential adults such as teachers. Teachers spend a good chunk of each day with students.

The answers to these questions led us to ask these last critical ones: *Couldn't we have a greater impact in the lives of students by finding ways to be more engaged in our community public schools rather than less engaged? Couldn't we have an impact in the lives of students if we could find ways to be more helpful to teachers, coaches, and staff rather than continually pointing out all the flaws in the system?*

We decided not to start our own school. We realized that if the Christian students, teachers, administrators, custodians, coaches, and lunchroom staff left the public schools, we were basically saying to those who remained, "You can go to hell."

We would love to tell you that our decision not to open our own school led the public school system to renounce various standards we don't like, that hundreds of public school employees have committed their lives to Christ, and that thousands of students in our district have discovered the difference a faith-based education can make. It wouldn't be true.

What *is* true is that each month hundreds of hours of work are being done by the people of LifeBridge in our schools. Each week, our Student Impact Ministry encourages students to find ways to express their faith in school through a variety of means. A few hundred teachers, coaches, and school staff are a part of the LifeBridge family. LifeBridge has found ways to serve the schools in our community and, in the serving, has created relationships that we believe are making a difference. Education *can* be faith-based, not just because of the curriculum, but because people of faith are teaching and leading students—even in the public school system. We can't count the number of times that Christian employees of our school district have thanked the people of our church for not abandoning them.

I have three children; the oldest two have recently graduated from our public school system. As parents, we weren't always pleased with what they were exposed to. We sometimes met with teachers and staff to discuss philosophy and practices. But even when we held opposing opinions, we were given a hearing and an opportunity to present a different perspective. Why? Because we had nurtured relationships with these people.

For several years members of our youth staff have been invited to come into the schools to teach in the health science classes on issues related to dating, sex, and values. One of our youth coaches began, through the church, an abstinence-based education program. This "Friends First" program was adopted by our school district and is now taught in many school districts around the country. These days, more than 500,000 students are receiving this abstinence-based program in public schools.[5] A local science teacher, who is a Christian, spent two years teaching Creation/Design theory classes at our church for interested students and parents. He was able to convince his high school to offer it as an elective class. These are just a few examples of the inroads that have been made as a result of our deliberate choice to be engaged in the lives of young people in public schools.

3. We decided to open our doors to other community organizations.

The church was once the heart of the community. But times have changed, and churches rarely get that opportunity now. In some cases, we have alienated ourselves, and in others, the community has alienated us. Controversy and the prevailing social climate have often put communities and congregations at odds.

When it was time for LifeBridge to seriously consider building a new facility, God gave us a broader vision than simply building a bigger building to house the people already in our church. Through a number of providential circumstances, our church was able to purchase over three hundred acres of undeveloped farmland in a growing area on the edge of our city. As we evaluated the church's needs, we also considered the needs of our rapidly growing community. We wanted to be at the heart of our community, not on its outskirts.

We did a lot of research before we even began to design the building or plan how to use the land. The church's leadership didn't do the research alone. We invited the entire church to answer the questions "What does our community need?" and "What are our church facility needs?" During twelve nights of brainstorming sessions, we covered tables with huge sheets of paper and, in small groups, church people thought about our county, city, schools, community, and neighborhoods. During those twelve nights, more than twelve hundred people from the church came up with over five thousand ideas for serving our community by being good stewards of our land.

> **More than twelve hundred people from the church came up with over five thousand ideas for serving our community by being good stewards of our land.**

At the same time, a task force from the church was meeting with nonprofits, city officials, health department officials, and county government representatives to ask, "What does our community need?" When we compared the lists, we found they shared many items. Many of those ideas are being incorporated into our new church campus. For us, being externally focused meant opening our facility to our community.

There were two immediate benefits to the brainstorming sessions. First, they gave the people of LifeBridge an opportunity to begin to ask, "What can we do for the community?" instead of "What can the church do for me?" Times of prayer and vision casting occurred throughout all of the brainstorming sessions. We often used the image of "crossing the street." For us at LifeBridge, that literally meant crossing the street from our church into the neighborhoods and city streets across the highway. It also means living out our faith where we work, live, and play. It has also come to mean serving. The brainstorming sessions became a catalyst for change for us.

The second immediate benefit was the new relationship that began to form between our church and the community. Of course, not every brainstorming session with community leaders was positive, but in the course of the conversations, trust began to develop.

In the end we realized that being good stewards of all God had provided meant using our space for more than a bigger church. It meant using part of our land to help address the growing housing needs of senior adults in our community. It meant planning our educational facilities so that they could be shared by the community college. It meant including parks and recreational facilities for the use of the entire community. It meant something as simple as providing meeting space. In the past year, hundreds of different groups and organizations have met at LifeBridge. These groups have included small and large business groups, public- and private-school groups, nonprofits, and civic groups.

Why have we opened our doors so wide? To be sure, putting out the welcome mat creates more work for our staff and cleaning crews, but it is one more way of staying externally focused. By opening our doors, we meet more people. Even through the bricks and sticks of our facility, we want to be good stewards of the gospel. ← ?? How ??

4. We decided that, to love and serve our community, we must know our community.

We became familiar with the real needs of our community instead of trying to fix what we perceived to be the problems. Just as you "don't fix it if it ain't broke," we learned that you can't fix it if you *don't know* it's broke. For us, serving in the community meant getting to know our community.

We began to learn a lot about our county that we hadn't known. We became familiar with the St. Vrain Community Council. This group's mission statement is "to improve the quality of life of individuals by coordinating resources and services in response to the social and economic needs of the community." This council is a unique association of individuals from non-profit agencies in the Longmont area who are dedicated to working together to meet our community's human-service needs. At their meetings, they share information and develop strategies to collectively reach their goals of serving Longmont residents. By attending their meetings, representatives of our church have seen that we are not alone in caring. A lot of groups in our community have a similar vision of serving people. Being a part of this council has given us a wealth of information and helped us develop important relationships.

A Closer Look

Homeless Students

In the summer of 2002, we were surprised to learn that there were 443 homeless students in our school district. Longmont, Colorado, is a nice place to live. People choose to move here, and our community is growing. New subdivisions are going up on all sides of town. Longmont doesn't look like it has homeless people. But it does. When the St. Vrain Community Council asked LifeBridge to help with a "Pack to School" program to help give these homeless students the school supplies they needed, we were happy to get involved. The program was a collaborative effort among the school district, the local Rotary club, several churches, the Salvation Army, and other non-profits. People at LifeBridge participated by donating supplies, specifically dictionaries and calculators. LifeBridge volunteers were also instrumental in both filling and delivering backpacks. Collectively, all of these organizations were able to meet the school-supply needs of our homeless students as they started back to school. This project also opened the door to addressing long-term issues related to homelessness. A number of initiatives have come from that.

5. We decided to invite everyone to jump into the stream!

Society is like a stream. If we don't like the direction it's going, we face a choice: We can either stand on the banks, yelling and screaming about what is wrong with the stream, or we can roll up our pant legs and wade in. We've decided at LifeBridge that we want to be among those who wade in to do whatever it takes to effect positive change.

Why should pastors have all the fun of ministry? Ministry and service are part of God's design for every follower of Jesus Christ. "For we are God's workmanship, created in Christ Jesus to do good works, which God prepared in advance for us to do" (Ephesians 2:10). If God has saved us "to do good works" which he has already prepared for us to do, and we are not engaged in those good works, no wonder most Christians feel unfulfilled! Pastors and vocational Christian workers shouldn't be the only ones who feel they have discovered the purpose for which they were created. Many people have significant ministries in addition to their professional occupations.

At LifeBridge, there are not very many hoops to jump through to be engaged in serving. From our ministry to children to our ministry to senior citizens, we make sure that there are service opportunities for all abilities and ages. There are projects for families, teenagers, senior adults, singles— anyone and everyone. Many of our members invite their non-Christian friends to help them serve. Everyone is encouraged to be involved in activities ranging from thinning trees to creating a fire line to serving in the kitchen of our local food bank. We offer short-term projects and ongoing service opportunities, but very few require participants to be members of LifeBridge.

A Closer Look   *Good one*

Middle School Students Make a Connection

They were skeptical at first, but after the first cleanup project, the residents of Grand Meadow Senior Citizens Trailer Park couldn't wait for the middle school students to return. With the help of parents, youth coaches, and the facility's manager, middle school students from LifeBridge Christian Church helped residents rake, trim, clean, paint, and repair their property.

This project began when a volunteer youth coach, Terry Haley, wanted students to see the difference they could make in the world right away. This Christmas service project was so successful that the middle school students now return once a quarter to help with seasonal cleaning. Though they were initially unsure about teenagers working on their homes, the residents now organize their project lists and bake cookies in preparation for the students' arrival. They even call the church to see when the students will be back. And of course, the middle school students benefit enormously from the experience. One of them commented, "It's so neat to be able to touch the hearts of these people and know that we are building friendships with them."

6. We decided to be open to innovative ideas and partnerships.

Initiating service opportunities is not the responsibility of only the church's leadership. We encourage everyone at every level of spiritual maturity to be involved in serving. In fact, serving is sometimes the first opportunity for involvement at LifeBridge Christian Church. We're also open to partnering with businesses and other groups to accomplish acts of service.

A Closer Look

The St. Genevieve Project

A number of years ago when the banks of the Mississippi were overflowing, our community, which was a thousand miles away, found a way to serve. It all started when a family from LifeBridge asked if they could invite their Bible study group to assist a family they knew in St. Genevieve, Missouri, who had lost their home. That request gave birth to asking our congregation to provide assistance to a church in St. Genevieve. We checked with other churches in our area to see if they wanted to help as well. In just a few days, several businesses decided to get involved too. In the end, the city of Longmont formed an official partnership with St. Genevieve to offer relief to that flooded city.

Every Wednesday for several months, a tractor-trailer load or two would leave Longmont with all kinds of supplies: clothing, construction materials, mechanical equipment, food, and other necessities. Those trailers were headed to St. Genevieve. On Thursdays and Fridays, United Airlines provided free seats on flights into the area for volunteers from Longmont who would then spend the weekend cleaning, rebuilding, and doing whatever was needed in St. Genevieve. This lasted for months. Schoolchildren got involved by sending supplies, and businesses sent supplies and gave people time off to help the people of St. Genevieve. Nearly every sector of the community found a way to respond.

Christians and non-Christians served side by side to aid people in St. Genevieve. It started because someone wanted to help someone else and the church leaders said, "Go for it!"

The Results of an External Focus

As we moved outside the walls of our church, we weren't surprised that the lives of those we were serving changed. But we were caught a little off guard by the community's receptivity, the eagerness with which people volunteered their time and energy, and the resulting changes in *their* lives. As each new opportunity to serve is created, another group of people wants to use that opportunity to serve and minister. Eventually we expect to have 100 percent of our people engaged in ministry outside of LifeBridge because they have found a way to serve that ignites their passion.

Changing our focus has also led to growth in a number of areas. In 1996 we had eleven hundred members. Today LifeBridge has three thousand worshipping each weekend in five services. Over the last several years, 80 percent of our new members were unchurched or de-churched people. We are excited about these statistics. But beyond numbers, LifeBridge is being salt and light in our city and surrounding communities. We are seeing both personal transformation and community transformation.

Jesus invites all of us to be salt and light:

Let me tell you why you are here. You're here to be salt-seasoning that brings out the God-flavors of this earth. If you lose your saltiness, how will people taste godliness? You've lost your usefulness and will end up in the garbage. Here's another way to put it: You're here to be light, bringing out the God-colors in the world. God is not a secret to be kept. We're going public with this, as public as a city on a hill. If I make you light-bearers, you don't think I'm going to hide you under a bucket, do you? I'm putting you on a light stand. Now that I've put you there on a hilltop, on a light stand— shine! Keep open house; be generous with your lives. By opening up to others, you'll prompt people to open up with God, this generous Father in heaven (Matthew 5:13-16, *The Message*).

We believe that when we are available to do what God does, we become his hands and his feet—salt and light in a world that needs salt and light.

"You're not worth your salt." That statement comes from a time in history when people were paid a day's wages in salt. In fact, in Jesus' day, Roman soldiers received their weekly wages in measures of salt. Before there were notary publics, it was common for people to sit down and share a portion of salt together after they struck a deal. It was a way of saying, "This is a binding agreement between us."

Jesus uses this common but essential item to say, "You are to be a preservative, an enhancer, and you are to bring value to the world." So LifeBridge is always asking, "Are we enhancing our community? Are we worth our salt?"

God has also commissioned Christians to be light. What would the world be like without light? Light illuminates; light attracts; light dispels the darkness. It's been said that the most important light in a house isn't the expensive chandelier. It's the little nightlight in the hallway. Why? Because that's the one that prevents you from stubbing your toe in the middle of the night. It illuminates a path. It dispels darkness. Sometimes our churches don't need to do extravagant things to make a real difference in the world. Sometimes we are most effective when we softly rub shoulders as we serve others.

For two years, LifeBridge members helped clean toilets and paint hallways at local elementary schools during Christmas break. Recently we were invited into kindergarten classrooms to help the kids make crafts. At the same school in which we had cleaned toilets for two years, we are now able to have a direct impact on the students and the teachers. Last year when a local high school student took his life, the school principal called LifeBridge. He asked if we could send over some staff and volunteer youth coaches for three days to be with the students on campus. How did LifeBridge gain such access to a public high school? We simply sent the same people who had been setting up chairs at assemblies, chaperoning the dances, and raking the long-jump pit all year.

When we put ourselves in the position of servants, God provides opportunities for ministry. Sometimes we want to help people without getting too close to them. But to show and model love, we have to get close to those we serve, even when it isn't comfortable or clean. In *A Place to Land*, Martha Manning wrote, "[Once] my idea of a perfect charity was to help people without actually having anything to do with them."[6]

To show and model love, we have to get close to those we serve, even when it isn't comfortable or clean.

Mother Teresa said it like this: "I am a little pencil in the hand of a writing God who is sending a love letter to the world." And we have the power to allow God to write his message of love through our service. Recently someone from our school district said, "We really appreciate LifeBridge because of all the things you do in the community, whether it's at the Inn Between [a transitional housing program] or helping out the homeless in our community or just being helpful where you can."

Jesus invited our churches to be salt and light. They're common things, really. There's nothing mystical, magical, or intricate about salt or light. Yet Jesus asks us to be churches of significance and influence and to make a difference in the environments we're in.

Something to **Think** About

Howard Hendricks once said, "I've never met a Christian who planned to live a mediocre life, but I have met plenty of mediocre Christians."

Something to **Talk** About

1. Is your church guilty of mediocrity?
2. What aspect of the LifeBridge story do you identify with?
3. What are your church's current outreach focus and methods?

Something to **Act** Upon

Make a list of ways your church is currently salt and light in your community.

Sermon/**Lesson** Idea

Text: Matthew 5:13-16

Main Idea: There are two ways that Christians lose their impact in a community. One way is by losing their "saltiness"—their distinctive flavor as believers. They become like everyone around them, or they are distinguished by all the things they are *against* rather than the things they are *for*—love, mercy, compassion, and service. The second way Christians lose their impact is by hiding their light. Though they are positive reflections of Jesus, their distinctiveness is hidden under a bowl—it is confined inside the four walls of the church. To have an impact, we must be both salt and light.

Illustration: The LifeBridge story

Action Points: What will you do to increase your "saltiness"—to become more distinctively Christlike in your values and actions? What will you do to become light—"[to] let your light shine before men, that they may see your good deeds and praise your Father in heaven"?

Endnotes

1. Walter Bagehot, *Physics and Politics*. Quoted in Everett M. Rogers, *Diffusion of Innovations* (New York: The Free Press, 1995), 335.

2. www.hubblesite.org

3. Joe S. Ellis, *The Church on Target* (Cincinnati, OH: Standard Publishing, 1986).

4. Howard Hendricks, comments (Ft. Lauderdale, FL: "Managing Your Time" seminar sponsored by World Vision, Marc Management, 1983).

5. www.friendsfirst.org

6. Martha Manning, *A Place to Land* (New York: Ballantine Books, 2003), as excerpted in Readers Digest (September 2003), 128.

chapter three

The **Power** of **Service**

"Jesus gave us a new norm of greatness...He who is greatest among you shall be your servant. That's a new definition of greatness...You only need a heart full of grace, a soul generated by love."

—Martin Luther King Jr. [1]

Service as a Hallmark

If you have ever had the pleasure of staying at a Ritz-Carlton hotel, you know it is one amazing experience. From the moment one arrives, each staff member is mindful of one thing: serving guests. The hotel chain's corporate motto is "We are ladies and gentlemen serving ladies and gentlemen." Serving doesn't happen by chance. Employees are genuinely empowered to correct a problem or handle a complaint. Stories describing the lengths to which staff members have gone to serve customers are legendary. When a guest thanks a wait person, chambermaid, or concierge, rather than responding, "Hey, it's OK" or "No problem," the employee looks the guest in the eye and with a smile responds, "It's a pleasure to serve you." Service like that is winsome. Little wonder that Ritz-Carlton is a perennial recipient of the hotel industry's most prestigious awards.[2] This company understands the power of service.

Why is service so powerful? Why does service accomplish so much good?

Is it really possible that communities can be transformed through service? To understand the power of service requires a deep understanding of three intersecting circles that form a visual construct for the externally focused church. Wherever churches are engaged in community transformation, the avenue they've chosen lies at the intersection of the *needs and dreams of the city or community, the mandates and desires of God, and the calling and capacity of the church*.

Picture three circles. The first circle represents—

The Needs and Dreams of the City

Every city has not only needs, which are usually obvious, but also aspirations...dreams of what it would like to become. How do we discover the needs and dreams of the city? The quickest way is simply to ask those who are in a position to know, that is, those who are actively serving the city—servants in law enforcement, fire protection, schools, public service, and so on.

Needs and Dreams of the City

For the past few years, the Boulder County ministerial alliance has been inviting leaders who serve our city to monthly luncheons. We've hosted our mayor, the president of the University of Colorado, the district attorney, the chief of police, the superintendent of schools, the city manager, the fire department chief, and others. When we asked these guests what they were trying to accomplish, none of them said, "Well, we'd really like to see more drug use, more liquor stores, an increased dropout rate, plummeting school test scores, more homelessness, and the pollution of Boulder Creek." On the contrary, apart from our spiritual aspirations, their view of a healthy city corresponds with our view of a healthy city—the kind of place we'd love to live in, to raise our families in. Consider your dreams for your city; most likely, most people in your city share them.

The Mandates and Desires of God

The second circle represents what God wants for a healthy city. Does God care about cities? Absolutely! How do we know what God wants for a city?

How do we discover his mandates and desires? In the Bible there are hundreds and hundreds of passages about cities. God wants cities to be safe places but also places of salvation. The Scriptures tell us that God can "watch over a city" (Psalm 127:1), that God can "bring health and healing" to a city (Jeremiah 33:6), and that transformed cities (because they have been cleansed and forgiven of their sins) can be a vehicle for bringing glory and honor to God: "Then this city will bring me renown, joy, praise and honor before all nations on earth that hear of all the good things I do for it; and they will be in awe and will tremble at the abundant prosperity and peace I provide for it" (Jeremiah 33:9).

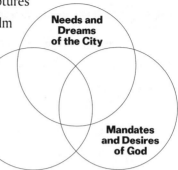

Jesus himself expressed his desire for the city to come into a saving relationship with himself: "O Jerusalem, Jerusalem…how often I have longed to gather your children together, as a hen gathers her chicks under her wings, but you were not willing!" (Luke 13:34). During Jesus' triumphal entry into Jerusalem, "as he approached Jerusalem and saw the city, he wept over it and said, 'If you, even you, had only known on this day what would bring you peace…'" (Luke 19:41-42). While the crowd was shouting joyful praise, Jesus was weeping for the city because it refused the life that he offered.

From Isaiah 65:17-25, Dr. Raymond Bakke, speaking of a future city, outlines six characteristics of a healthy community from the heart of God.

- public celebrations and happiness (verses 17-25)
- public health for children and [the] aged (verse 20)
- housing for all (verse 21)
- food for all (verse 22)
- family support systems (verse 23)
- absence of violence (verse 25)[3]

To this list we would add

- meaningful work (verses 22-23).

That's a pretty good starting place, isn't it? Isn't that the kind of city you would like to live in?

The Calling and Capacity of the Local Church

The church has a place in creating healthy, transformed communities. Churches don't have the luxury of withdrawing from the community. Whether they feel wanted or not, churches must realize that the community cannot be healthy, and all that God wants it to be, without their active engagement and involvement in its life—that's the way God designed it.

God has always used his people to bring hope and health to a community. Ezra and Nehemiah were wonderful restorers of the city. God-followers have always had the privilege of working in partnership with God to care for the widow, the orphan, the alien, the disabled, and the poor. Part of the calling of the church is to minister to the disenfranchised. Aristides, a Christian apologist in first-century Athens, described Christians to the Roman Emperor Hadrian this way: "They love one another. They never fail to help widows; they save orphans from those who would hurt them. If they have something they give freely to the man who has nothing; if they see a stranger, they take him home, and are happy, as though he were a real brother." [4]

In addition to showing mercy and love as a reflection of the character of God, God has called the church to bring the gospel to and disciple all nations (Matthew 28:18-20; Mark 16:15). Today people from many nations have come to our cities and communities, and God has mandated that the church bring the gospel to our communities. The calling of the church is clear.

The capacity of each local church determines the part it will play as an agent of community transformation. No church can do it all, but every church has the capacity to serve the city and the people of the community in a meaningful way that represents the love, mercy, and power of God.

Looking at the Intersections

The most interesting part of this visual construct are the intersections where the city, God, and the church meet. While the circles represent the different entities, the intersections describe what happens between these entities. *"Common grace" is the term we use to describe the space where the interests of the city intersect with the desires of God (apart from the church).* This is actually John Calvin's term, which he used to describe that which God wants to do for a city that he doesn't need the church to accomplish.[5] Common grace is God's beneficence toward everyone as reflected in Luke 6:35: "[God] is kind to the ungrateful and wicked" and Matthew 5:45: "He causes his sun to rise on the evil and the good, and sends rain on the right-eous and the unrighteous." God desires for

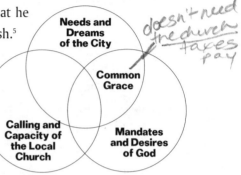

doesn't need the church taxes pay

all people to live in safety and with justice. The city wall that provides protection for believer and unbeliever is an expression of common grace. Common grace includes public works such as schools, streetlights, traffic lights, sewers, roads, and bridges. Common grace also includes public services such as police and fire protection. Calvin said we pay our taxes to procure common grace.[6] Common grace is part of the reason we "give to Caesar what is Caesar's" (from Mark 12:17).

"Control" is the intersection between the city and the church (apart from the will of God).

either way not good

The history of this intersection has generally not been a good one. Some European states have exerted control over the church. Here in the United States, there has been a well-intentioned, though often checkered, history of the church trying to control the policies of the state. In either case, control on the part of either entity has not led to a sustained impact for the gospel.

"Salvation" is the intersection of what God wants for the city and what the church has the calling and capacity to do in relation to the city—to bring salvation to the city.

The Scripture passage that best describes this intersection is 1 Timothy 2:1-7, in which we are called to intercede, pray, and give thanks for our leaders and to actively work toward bringing salvation to the city because God "wants all men to be saved and to come to a knowledge of the truth" (1 Timothy 2:4). God's words to the exiles who were carried off to Babylon are also relevant here: "Seek the peace and prosperity of the city to which I have carried you into exile. Pray to the Lord for it, because if it prospers, you too will prosper" (Jeremiah 29:7).

Now note something else from the intersecting circles. As much as God wants the city to be saved and the task of saving the people of the city is the calling of the church, salvation is really outside of what the city desires. Interestingly, none of the city officials we asked to describe a healthy Boulder included a desire to see the city saved. So our strategies to introduce our city to Christ have historically involved either inviting people out of the city into our churches where they can hear the gospel, or bringing a gospel event into the city. Both of these strategies may have been effective in the past, but what about the future? How can we gain entrance to the city? That brings us to our fourth intersection.

The Transformational "Sweet Spot"

"Service" is the only location that encompasses the needs and dreams of the city, the mandates and desires of God, and the calling and capacity of the church. Service is the "sweet spot" where all three interests come together. Service is something the community needs, God desires, and the church has the capacity to do. The community may not care much about salvation, but it does have needs. It is in meeting those needs through service that meaningful relationships develop, and out of relationships come endless opportunities to share

share the gospel

the love of Christ and the gospel of salvation. The early church grew because its people loved and served. We believe servants can go anywhere. Service gives us access not only to places of need but also to places of influence.

Increasingly we have found that in areas of ministry we never could have forced our way into, we are now being invited to serve, and that service has become a bridge to salvation. It is "God's kindness" that leads to repentance (Romans 2:4), not the threat of God's judgment. Barriers to the gospel melt away when people are served and blessed. It's been said, "There is only one way to God and that is through Jesus. But there are a thousand ways to Jesus." By creating a thousand entry points into the community, we create a thousand opportunities to show the love and share the good news with the city.

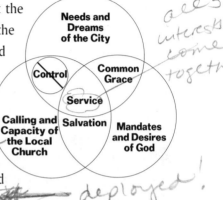

1000 ways

all 3 interests come together

deployed!

As we have entered into the life of the city through service, we have had the opportunity to engage with people from whom we normally would be isolated. We are seeing relationships formed and people taking steps toward God and his church as never before. Good deeds form a great bridge over which the good news can travel! The doors to salvation have opened through service. People from the community have asked our churches to start churches in nursing homes, to mentor juvenile offenders, to serve as chaplains in nonprofit agencies, to work with the homeless, to work in schools, and to serve in many other environments into which we never could have forced our way.

Selfless service gets everyone's attention. In the autumn of 2003, twenty-five students and a few adults from one church in our community did something rarely seen in Boulder—they went to local businesses and raked leaves, cleaned toilets, and washed customers' windshields without accepting any money in return. When people asked, "Why do you want to do this?" they simply replied, "We just want to show you God's love in a practical way." Many people said, "This is really cool." After having his wind-shield washed, one man who had just arrived in town said, "I'm taking this idea back to Pennsylvania and telling the people there what the people in Boulder are doing." One business owner responded, "You won't believe this, but we were just praying for someone to come and clean our toilet!" During the afternoon, these young servants had the opportunity to share the gospel with individuals who asked to know more. Servants get invited to places into which the mighty can't force their way.

Servants get invited to places into which the mighty can't force their way.

When people come to faith, they can immediately be involved in serving others. From the get-go, they can understand that being a Christian isn't an isolated experience but a life lived in community and service.

Mission Arlington sees hundreds of people come to Christ each year. In 2002 this group welcomed over sixteen hundred new believers into the family of God. Lives are being touched. Lives are being changed. Many who have come to know Jesus Christ now serve as volunteers. Service is not only the bridge to salvation, but salvation is also the bridge to service.

A Closer Look

Mission Arlington

Mission Arlington is a house-church movement that operates in the space where God's desires, the city's dreams, and the church's capacity intersect. It is fully engaged in the sweet spot of service. A remarkable woman named Tillie Burgin started Mission Arlington. For several years Tillie had served as a missionary in Korea but eventually found herself in Arlington, Texas, working as a school administrator. In 1986 Tillie saw the needs around her and asked herself, "Why can't we treat Arlington as a mission field?" And so she did. Her mission was simple: to take the church to the people who were not going to church, "to hang out and hover around John 3:16." As she ventured out to meet and minister to her neighbors, she was immediately challenged by Jehovah's Witnesses who told her, "You're invading our territory. Get back into your church building where you belong." Fortunately for Arlington, Tillie did not listen, and little by little, ministries began.

Today Mission Arlington comprises nearly 250 community house churches (with nearly four thousand people in attendance) serving thousands of people a week in the Arlington community by offering such things as food, clothing, furniture, school supplies, medical and dental care, school transportation, child and adult day care, after-school programs for eleven hundred kids at forty-six locations, counseling, conversational English, citizenship classes, and job assistance. Mission Arlington even offers a room where the underemployed who work nights can catch a few winks during the day. Although the square-block ministry center is burgeoning with love and compassion, the real ministry takes place in the 247 house churches scattered in homes and apartments around Arlington.

Each day hundreds of people come through the center with various types of needs. After those needs are met, the geographically appropriate house churches follow up with them. Last Thanksgiving, the people of Mission Arlington fed nearly eleven hundred people *in their own homes*, having realized that people would rather eat with families and friends than in a "center" somewhere. This is just one example of how Tillie and her co-workers treat all people with kindness and dignity. In 2003 more than twenty-one thousand people came through Mission Arlington's Christmas store, heard the Christmas story (more than eight hundred people indicated that they made salvation decisions at that time), and then selected gifts (new or nearly new products provided by local merchants and individuals) they would not otherwise have been able to afford. One little boy chose a brooch and then had it wrapped as a gift for his mother. He was seen unwrapping it and then getting back in line with the same brooch to have it wrapped again. This cycle was repeated a few times. Finally Tillie asked him what in the world he was doing. He said he had never been treated as nicely as those people were treating him and so he got in line just to feel the love!

The Full Extent of Our Love

On the night before his trial and crucifixion, Jesus met with his disciples for the Passover meal. John records that although Jesus had always loved his disciples, he now did something to *show them* the "full extent of his love" (John 13:1). Did you catch that? He always loved his disciples, but now he wanted to *show* them exactly how much he loved them. So what did he do? He didn't invite them to come to church to hear a speaker or see a program. He simply served the disciples by washing and drying their feet before they ate the evening meal. The disciples knew that Jesus loved them because he served them. The way that Jesus demonstrated love was through service. The lesson? "Now that I, your Lord and Teacher, have washed your feet,

> **No act of service is too menial to be without meaning.**

you also should wash one another's feet. I have set you an example that you should do as I have done for you" (John 13:14-15). Jesus served those who would become servants, who in turn would serve others, who would become servants. The emergence of externally focused churches proves that this lesson has survived the journey to the twenty-first century.

Service is always about meeting others' needs or helping others succeed. Service puts the needs of others at least on a par with our own. Service happens in that delightful intersection where something that needs to be done is met by someone who is ready, willing, and able to do it. Selfless, self-forgetting service is what opens the hearts of people. When Jesus asked the blind beggar, "What do you want me to do for you?" (Luke 18:41), he was demonstrating the heart of a servant. He was asking the question all true servants ask. When Jesus washed the disciples' feet or made a fire and prepared a breakfast of fish and bread after a morning of fishing (John 21:9), he was showing his disciples that no act of service is too menial to be without meaning.

Service is the action that causes us to move toward others in love. Service is the mark of the Christian. We are to have the same attitude about service as Jesus had and still has: "Your attitude should be the same as that of Christ Jesus...taking the very nature of a servant" (Philippians 2:5-7).

Mosaic pastor Erwin McManus writes, "There is something mystical about servanthood because God is a servant. When we serve others, we more fully reflect the image of God, and our hearts begin to resonate with the heart of God. We may never be more like God than when we're serving from a purely selfless motivation."[7]

Servanthood is not one of the spiritual gifts. We are never exempt from service because we "don't have that gift." In fact, the Apostle Peter writes that "each one should use whatever gift he has received *to serve others*" (1 Peter 4:10a, emphasis added). The Scriptures record that people came to

Servanthood is not one of the spiritual gifts. We are never exempt from service because we "don't have that gift."

Jesus "to hear him and to be healed of their diseases" (Luke 5:15; 6:18), but Jesus had more than that on his agenda. Matthew 20:28 records that Jesus came "to serve and to give." Many followers of Jesus today also think that church is a place to hear God's Word and be healed of their diseases. But will the church also be a place of serving and giving? Will it be your place of serving and giving?

The Paradox of Incarnational Ministry

Much is written and said today about an "incarnational" approach to ministry—where we move beyond words and try to embody the message we are proclaiming. When we think of "incarnational ministry," we naturally think of Jesus, the incarnate Christ—the complete revelation of God to the lost world (John 1:14). We hear the exhortation from the pulpit: "You know, you may be the only gospel that people ever see; you may be the only Bible they will ever read. You need to become Jesus to these people." And it probably makes us feel good to think that we are like Jesus when we love and serve others. Jesus does talk about incarnating himself in the lives of people. However, maybe not in *us*!

In Matthew 25:35-46 Jesus talks about this. "For I was hungry and you gave me something to eat, I was thirsty and you gave me something to drink, I was a stranger and you invited me in, I needed clothes and you clothed me, I was sick and you looked after me, I was in prison and you came to visit me."

His followers are confused and respond by asking, "Lord, when did we see you hungry and feed you, or thirsty and give you something to drink? When did we see you a stranger and invite you in, or needing clothes and clothe you? When did we see you sick or in prison and go to visit you?"

Then Jesus replies, "I tell you the truth, whatever you did for one of the least of these brothers of mine, you did for me." It is not those to whom we minister who meet Jesus in a ministry encounter; it is the ones who are doing the ministering! *We're not Jesus to them. They are Jesus to us!* Notice Jesus doesn't say, "*as if* you were doing it to me," which would imply a metaphor. He says, "You were doing it to me." Mother Teresa described her ministry strategy as going out and looking for the dying, the cripple, the lonely, the unwanted, the unloved—"Jesus in disguise." Are we willing to find him?

A Look at the Scriptures

Scores of Scripture passages describe God's heart for the underserved in a community. In the Old Testament, God's heart for the poor, the alien, the widow, the orphan, and the needy is clearly revealed as he tells his people to be the advocates of the unfortunate. The Scriptures always inform us of the way things ought to be from God's perspective. They give us a glimpse into his heart and the kind of heart he wants to give us. When people understand the Scriptures and what God wants them to do, their lives are transformed. Externally focused churches that are salt and light in their communities have strong scriptural convictions regarding their ministry outside the walls of the church. See the Appendix (p. 219) for a list of Scriptures revealing God's heart for the disenfranchised.

The Good Samaritan

The Samaritan (Luke 10:30-37) did a number of practical things to be a neighbor to the poor soul who was waylaid outside Jerusalem. *First, the good Samaritan didn't avoid the person in need.* Most ministry opportunities that God puts in front of us happen at the intersection of the unexpected and the interruption. "By chance" is the operative phrase in this story.

Second, the Samaritan offered medical help. Medical and dental costs have soared in recent years. Is there anything you can do to offer medical or dental care for the needy of your community? A couple of years ago, Mariners Church in Irvine, California, was ministering to a teenage boy through their partnership with Orange County Social Services Foster Care. He was a good kid but painfully shy and withdrawn, mostly due to severe acne and the accompanying scarring. Mariners covered the cost of the laser surgery and treatment that made his skin like that of a newborn baby.[8] Do you think that made a difference in the life of a teenager? Do you think he'll ever forget the kindness shown to him by believers?

Third, the Samaritan provided transportation by putting the wounded man on his donkey. One of the ways the poor are isolated is through a lack of public transportation. If those without automobiles can't get to work or to school, they can't climb out of poverty. Arlington Texas, for example, has virtually no public transportation. Unless you have access to a car, it's tough to get around. So Mission Arlington began a public transportation ministry that hauls more than two thousand people a day to work and to school. Maybe it's a bit ambitious to start a bus company, but there are other ways of helping with transportation. Is there anything your church could do to take shut-ins grocery shopping or to doctor appointments?

Many churches are discovering that free oil changes are an excellent foray into the community. LifeBridge Christian Church will have a two-bay garage in its new facility for auto service priced on a sliding scale.

Calvary Bible Evangelical Free Church in Boulder, Colorado, has an annual bike tune-up clinic in three local parks. When a single mom showed up with her dilapidated bike (her only means of transportation), the men didn't have the parts or tools to tune up such an antique. So the men from the church took her bike to the local bike shop and within an hour had the bike tuned like new. In the face of such kindness, the woman cried.

Dave Workman, lead pastor of Vineyard Community Church in Cincinnati, Ohio, says, "It takes between twelve and twenty positive bumps [refreshing encounters with the church] before people come to Christ."[9] Our presence in the public square through service gives us opportunities to provide these "refreshing encounters."

Fourth, the Samaritan provided lodging and companionship. He actually took the injured man to an inn and stayed with him throughout the darkest hours of the night. Three years ago Calvary Bible in Boulder responded to a request from a homeless shelter to provide overflow housing on the coldest nights of the year. The church responded by hosting eight to ten men every Monday night from October to April. Calvary Bible recognizes that homelessness is not a disease; it simply describes a person's relationship to permanent housing.

A Closer Look

Recognizing Christ

Last spring my friend Donny and I (Eric) volunteered to pick up ten men from the homeless shelter and take them to the church to spend the night. After picking them up in the church van, we drove back to the church, where we set out some snacks and then watched *Dumb and Dumber* together before praying for the men, setting up cots in the gym, and turning in for the night. Because the men had to leave by 7 o'clock the next morning, Donny got up at 4:30 and fixed his "All-Time Cinnamon Rolls," which he normally bakes only on Christmas morning. After awaking to the smell of hot coffee and oven-fresh cinnamon rolls laden with icing and butter, the men soon lined up in the kitchen. One by one they opened their lives to us and to one another.

Both Donny and I had recently studied the Matthew 25 passage regarding meeting Jesus through the poor and needy. Watching the men as they gobbled down the best cinnamon rolls they had ever eaten, I asked Donny what he was thinking. "I was just thinking, 'Jesus sure likes cinnamon rolls.' "

Is there anything you can do to provide lodging or companionship to any of the least of these? Can you simply volunteer at the local shelter? Can your church provide shelter? Can you swing a hammer to help build a Habitat for Humanity house?

It's interesting that *the last thing the Samaritan offered was money* (which he gave to the innkeeper). So much good can be done apart from money. Vicki Baird, director of MercyWorks of Cincinnati's Vineyard Community Church says that "the poor need relationships more than they need money. In the inner city, there's a lot of free stuff to be had. What the poor need is people who care."[10] And she's probably right. But sometimes there is no substitute for cash—the tool of tools. Cash is necessary to pay for medical expenses and heating bills. One church in Boulder even helped an Iranian immigrant with a modest down payment on a house! This is the love of Christ made visible.

A Closer Look

Creekside Community Church

A few years ago, John Bruce, pastor of Creekside Community Church of San Leandro, California, met with the principal of an elementary school in Oakland. He asked what the church could do to help the school. At the time, violence in this school was so bad that sometimes half the kids were absent simply because they didn't want to get beaten up. The church responded by providing men to be present on the playgrounds during recess and during the lunch hour.

School attendance rose, so the church began looking for other opportunities to serve. They determined that they could have the greatest impact by working with the bottom 10 percent of elementary school students. By working with this group, they hope to raise the level of education for the entire school system. By working one-on-one with students in the classroom and with groups of students after class—assisting them with homework, playing with them, and providing learning games—members of this church are creating an atmosphere in which students can learn and thrive.

Beyond helping students, the volunteers from Creekside support and serve the teachers by providing breakfast, recognition ceremonies, gift bags, praise, and appreciation. The principal was quick to point out that "these activities went a long way toward maintaining teacher morale during the difficult times of this past school year. When they feel appreciated and valued, teachers provide a higher level of service to our students."

But What If Nothing Happens?

Sometimes we ask ourselves, "But what if we serve and nothing happens? What if we do all this stuff for people and they don't respond?" One pastor friend confessed that one of the hardest things about his church's "Adopt-a-Block" ministry is to work all Saturday cleaning a neighbor's yard without being thanked. While some people will say they've never experienced such love before, some will indeed receive Christ, and some will even become vibrant leaders in the church, a lot of people will simply have no response to your service. But it's OK. It has all happened before.

Jesus knelt by the tub of soapy water. "Having loved his own...he now showed them the full extent of his love" (John 13:1b). He would wash and dry his disciples' feet, his last recorded act of service before going to the Cross. What did one have to do to deserve a foot washing? Have faith? If so, Jesus should have skipped Thomas. Demonstrate loyalty? Well, then he should have passed by Peter. Behave honestly? Then he should certainly skip Judas, the one who would betray him. No, he would wash the feet of all because the act was about Jesus, not them. Service is only truly service when it is done without the expectation of a payback.

Knowing that only one of the ten lepers whom he would heal would return to give thanks did not prevent Jesus from healing the other nine. Healing was what the Father called him to do, whether people thanked him or not. One day Jesus would surrender himself to the hammer and nails that pinned him to the cross. He would willingly give his all so that all could believe and have eternal life. Did he know that not all would believe? Did that prevent him from dying for our sins? The Apostle Paul reminds us, "Let us not become weary in doing good, for at the proper time we will reap a harvest if we do not give up. Therefore, as we have opportunity, let us do good to all people" (Galatians 6:9-10a).

No Good Deed Goes Unpunished

A friend of ours, former Boulder Chief of Police Tom Koby, often observes, "No good deed goes unpunished," and he's more right than wrong. Many people have a vested interest in the status quo, and your ministry of changing lives will interrupt their worlds. Not all people you serve will respond. Worse yet, the very ones who are the beneficiaries of your service may turn on you. But it's all happened before, and if we want to follow the footsteps of Jesus, we must follow the same path Jesus walked. After Jesus had healed a man with a shriveled hand, Luke tells us that the Pharisees, rather than being excited, "were furious and began to discuss with one another what they might do to Jesus" (Luke 6:11). Peter and John were "called to account...for an act of kindness shown to a cripple" (Acts 4:9). We'd like to think that our ministry to others will always result in repentance, conversion, and admiration, but it doesn't. However, that shouldn't keep us from loving and serving, because that is the calling of the Christian.

A Closer Look

Lifeboat 14

On April 14, 1912, the *Titanic* struck an iceberg in the North Atlantic and began taking on water. By the time the lifeboats were deployed, it was clear that the ship was sinking. Passengers were loaded into lifeboats, and the lifeboats were lowered into the icy waters. Of the twenty lifeboats lowered into the water, most had room for more people. Despite the cries for help, those in the lifeboats were afraid to return to the drowning people lest the boats be swamped. Resisting the cries for help, the people in the boats rowed away from hundreds of people floating in the water.

In Lifeboat 14, Fifth Officer Harold Lowe thought differently and acted differently. He transferred many of his passengers to other lifeboats and returned to the sinking ship to pick up more survivors. Though he could not save them all, he could save a precious few from death in the icy sea. Survivors rescued survivors.[11]

At Colorado Community Church (CCC) in Aurora, Colorado, Lifeboat 14 has become a metaphor for externally focused ministry. Although the people of CCC care for those in the boat, they are defined by going after those who are still in the water. They are a group of "transformed people transforming people." So "church" is not just what happens on Sunday morning at their Aurora facility. Pastor Robert Gelinas describes CCC's mission as

- connecting people to Christ,
- connecting people to a community, and
- connecting people to their calling.

Their strategy of "weaving a fabric of friendship" with the community takes many innovative forms. They seek to make the gospel "accessible in holistic and culturally relevant ways" to every person in their community. Through "Operation Church on the Block," CCC takes the church to the streets in order to bring Christ's love to those who live in low-income areas. The church rents apartments in complexes along the main traffic corridors of its community in order to bring the church to the people. "An apartment in every apartment building, a trailer in every trailer park. That's our goal," says Pastor Gelinas. The Church on the Block consists of Bible studies, fun activities, mentoring and tutoring of youth, and leadership and skills development.

On the first Sunday of each month, a "lifeboat offering" is taken to stock the church's resource center. This center is used to meet the needs of the folks in the apartments and trailer parks. The offering is based upon the needs that the people of CCC observe in the lives of those they serve, and it may include items such as canned goods, diapers, shampoo, and school supplies.

Recognizing that most people want to give to ministries outside the church, CCC employs what they call their "5+5" missions strategy. They ask their members to give 5 percent of their incomes to ministries outside of the church. Pastor Gelinas says, "We now have a missions committee of seventeen hundred—each one deciding where God is working, and investing in it." [12] The faith of the people of CCC is lived out in the community. They get involved in the dreams and hurts of their community. They don't condemn. They love and serve. They don't retreat; they go after those still in the water. The *Titanic* remains at the bottom of the Atlantic, but Lifeboat 14 is still involved in pulling people out of the water in Aurora, Colorado.

Something to **Think** About

"He defended the cause of the poor and needy, and so all went well. Is that not what it means to know me?" (Jeremiah 22:16).

Something to **Talk** About

1. Why are we often so hesitant to serve?

2. Would your church be called a "serving church"? Why or why not?

3. What do you think Erwin McManus meant when he wrote, "We may never be more like God than when we're serving"?

4. How can serving the city be a bridge to salvation?

5. How can salvation be a bridge to serving the city?

Something to **Act** Upon

Study and seek to understand these Scriptures.

- Jeremiah 29:4-7
- Jeremiah 33:6-9
- Isaiah 58:1-8
- Isaiah 65:17-25
- Luke 13:34
- Luke 19:41
- Luke 6:36
- Matthew 5:45

Sermon/**Lesson** Idea

Text: Luke 10:30-37

Main Idea: Ministry often takes place at the intersection of need and "chance." In this story of the good Samaritan, the behavior of the two religious leaders is contrasted with that of the Samaritan. Discuss the practical ways the Samaritan provided practical assistance to the victim.

Illustration: Practical ways churches described in this chapter have creatively met the physical needs of others in their communities

Action Point: Invite the principal of a local grammar school to describe the needs and dreams of the school as well as your church's opportunities to serve that school.

Endnotes

1. Martin Luther King Jr., "The Drum Major Instinct," a sermon delivered at Ebenezer Baptist Church in Atlanta, Georgia, on February 4, 1968.

2. www.ritzcarlton.com

3. Ray Bakke, *A Theology as Big as the City* (Downers Grove, IL: InterVarsity Press, 1997), 82-83.

4. Aristides as quoted in *Loving God* by Charles W. Colson (Grand Rapids, MI: Zondervan Publishing House, 1983), 176.

5. Bakke, *A Theology as Big as the City,* 159.

6. Ibid.

7. Erwin Raphael McManus, *An Unstoppable Force* (Loveland, CO: Group Publishing, Inc., 2001), 175-176.

8. Laurie Beshore (of Mariner's Lighthouse Ministries), comments (Irvine, CA: conversation with Eric Swanson, March 25, 2003).

9. Dave Workman, comments (Cincinnati, OH: conversation with Eric Swanson, May 6, 2003).

10. Vicki Baird, comments (Cincinnati, OH: conversation with Eric Swanson, May 6, 2003).

11. www.titanic-online.com

12. Robert Gelinas, comments (Denver, CO: conversation with Eric Swanson, June 3, 2003).

chapter four

Helping **People Grow**

"God has created a new movement of churches that equip people, according to their calling and gifts, to be salt and light in their churches, communities, family, workplace, media, and government—in the whole of society."

—Kirbyjon Caldwell[1]

Diet Without Exercise

I (Eric) walked away from the breakfast buffet table with my plate piled high with bacon. The doctor's book had encouraged me to eat all the fat and protein I wanted, and a plate of bacon looked particularly good to me after a sumptuous breakfast of cheese omelets and pork sausage. Carnivore that I am, I thought, "Man, this is a great diet! Finally! A diet for a man with an appetite!" My friends scoffed at me, but I assured them that the diet and the science behind it were sound.

I ate some memorable meals while on this diet. One evening at the Capitol Grill in Washington, D.C., I treated myself to a large "surf and turf"—a well-marbled twenty-four-ounce steak along with a lobster tail fresh from Maine. If that were not enough fat and protein, I was also served a cup of pure, melted creamery butter to flavor my lobster. What butter wasn't absorbed by the lobster was put to good use as a condiment for my steak. I don't think the waiter had ever seen anyone polish off a cup of butter before. Apart from the minor chest pains, it was a great dinner. I felt like a combination of Jack Spratt and his wife—eating fat and lean with my platter clean.

Who needs exercise? As I strictly adhered to my protein and fat diet, I waited for the pounds to melt off. And while I was waiting, I figured I might as well have a few high-protein snacks. After all, proteins and fats are not the causes of weight gain; it's those darned carbohydrates. So, at work, I loaded the refrigerator with a whole ham and ten pounds of cheddar cheese. Throughout the day I'd make myself little ham and cheese sandwiches, alternating between the ham and the cheese serving as the bread. Although at night when I'd lie down, I'd picture the butter and cheese and bacon fat lodging in my arteries, I reassured myself with the thought that I'd soon be a lighter me. This was great until I got on the scales a couple of weeks later. Wow! I'd gained nine pounds! What a disappointment. So I got on the Web and discovered that 5 percent of the population does not respond favorably to this type of diet. Rats!

What's Your Growth Model?

All pastors consciously or subconsciously subscribe to a "growth" model or "spiritual formations" model in helping their congregations mature in faith. They know that the Bible has something to do with growth. After all, Jesus said, "Man does not live on bread alone, but on every word that comes from the mouth of God" (Matthew 4:4). Peter wrote about craving for "spiritual milk, so that by it you may grow up in your salvation" (from 1 Peter 2:2). And the author of Hebrews exhorts us to move from milk to "solid food" (Hebrews 5:14). So, as with my diet, if a little protein is good, then a lot must be great! As a result of this thinking, people are encouraged to not only listen to preaching on Sunday mornings but to also have a daily time in God's Word and to be part of a small-group Bible study. This growth model may be summarized like this: "Given enough time and truth, people will grow and change."

People need exercise for physical health and service for spiritual health.

But is the Bible, by itself, sufficient for spiritual health and spiritual growth? Good nutrition alone cannot make a person healthy. Good Bible teaching alone is insufficient for spiritual maturity. People need exercise for physical health and service for spiritual health. We learn from the Scriptures, but we grow by serving others.

The Apostle Paul made it fairly clear that his purpose was to "present everyone perfect in Christ" (from Colossians 1:28)—that every believer be mature, whole, complete in Christ, that everyone be mature in faith and character. Of course, this maturity is the result of a person's growing relationship with Christ. Helping people grow spiritually is an important part of each church's ministry. *Discipling, spiritual development, Christian maturity*—whichever term we choose, its objective is to present believers complete in Christ. Most churches hope that people will grow spiritually, share their faith, and be engaged in service.

How often have we heard the slogan "Bring them in; build them up; send them out"? Not a bad approach; it sounds logical and should work. But the leadership of LifeBridge Christian Church has found that many people don't get excited about spiritual disciplines. Like most churches, LifeBridge offers classes, small groups, and many other opportunities for spiritual development. Some people really jump at the chance to grow, while others are intimidated. The church also challenges its people to share their faith and to learn the skills to do so; but again, not as many as we'd like respond to the challenge.

Getting people involved in service is much easier than getting them involved in activities specifically designed to deepen their faith.

LifeBridge and other churches have discovered that getting people involved in service is much easier than getting them involved in activities specifically designed to deepen their faith. But they're also finding that people return from their service opportunities asking, "Can you teach me how to pray, understand the Bible, and share my faith? I was helping out at the food bank, and the person I was working with knew I was from the church and asked me to pray! I don't know how! Can you help me? I had an opportunity to share my faith, and I wasn't sure what to say. What should I do?"

In serving, people have all kinds of opportunities to have their faith stretched. Of course, it is possible to serve without growing spiritually, just as some people can stuff themselves full of knowledge and never really serve. If Christian maturity is our goal, then there must be many keys to unlocking a passion for spiritual growth. It seems in our culture today that service is an easier reach for people. In addition, serving puts people in real-world situations where their faith is on the line. People who may never have shown an interest in always having an answer for the hope that is within them (1 Peter 3:15) get excited when they are presented with that unexpected opportunity.

A Closer Look
Make a Difference Day

Several years ago, Christ's Church of the Valley (CCV) in Northwest Phoenix, Arizona, started a "CCV Make a Difference Day." In 2003, they mobilized 3,286 of their people to serve in a one-day community restoration project. Working with businesses, community leaders, and city officials, they identified 176 homes that needed painting, repair, or landscaping. Small groups were mobilized and deployed into the community, and by the end of the day they had used over two thousand gallons of paint and fifteen hundred tons of gravel to improve their community. CCV has found a simple way to mobilize its small groups into the community through acts of service. Involvement pastor Terry Anderson is excited about ministry opportunities for small groups, and CCV Make a Difference Day provides a simple, catalytic event in which nearly anyone can participate. Terry outlines four benefits of such an approach:

- Service gets small groups out of their comfort zones.
- Service causes groups to bond together in tighter relationships.
- Service is a vehicle for evangelistic opportunities.
- Service provides goodwill in the community. [2]

Another benefit of service is that there is often an immediate reward that motivates continued growth. People thrive on opportunities to give back to others, for their lives to make a difference, to positively influence the world around them, and to be a part of enhancing their community.

Wellspring of Living Water

A couple of years ago, a number of church leaders met to discuss externally focused ministry. They were seated in a circle, and one by one, they all had a chance to introduce themselves and tell their stories. One of the most interesting people there was Mary Frances Bowley, a gifted Bible study leader at Peachtree Baptist Church in Atlanta. Many women attended small groups at her church, and they were shocked when she told them that all small-group Bible studies for women were disbanded and could only reconstitute if they had a community ministry component.

So, according to Mary Frances, the women went to the "highways and hedges" of Atlanta to begin ministries to women no one else was reaching—cashiers, food service employees, hairdressers, single moms, women at the women's shelter, strippers, and prostitutes. When asked to explain her ministry's mission, she said, "To save the women of Atlanta."

There was a follow-up question: "You mean the strippers and the prostitutes?"

"No," she answered, "the women who are sitting in the pews of Atlanta every Sunday morning!"

What a shock! Mary Frances calls this ministry Wellspring of Living Water. The goal of Wellspring is to get the women within the church to reach the women outside the church. She firmly believes that people cannot grow into Christian maturity without giving themselves away to others. Mary Frances understands that for Christians to grow, nutrition is only half the equation. Exercise is the other half.

Making a Difference in L.A.

Mosaic in Los Angeles is all about being externally focused. The people of this church meet in three different locations, from a high school in East Los Angeles to a production theater in Hollywood. They have grown to be a church of fifteen hundred without parking! For the past four years, they have sent an average of one adult each month overseas as a career worker—mostly into the areas of China, Indonesia, India, the Middle East, and North Africa.

Lead pastor Erwin McManus has this to say about spiritual growth and service: "Some people believe that growth is like a series of steps—first you teach them for several months, then you put them in a training program for a while, then finally you give them some service opportunities. I don't believe that. I believe that as every baby is born with everything it will need as an adult, except in a smaller form, so, too, every child of God is reborn with everything he or she needs to grow and serve Christ. So from day one, and sometimes even *before* a person becomes a Christian, we get them serving in the community.

"In our home you're just a guest and don't become family until you take out the garbage."

"I may not know much about discipleship, but I do know this: Discipleship is not what happens *inside* the four walls of this church. We've also discovered that the biggest factor in our church's retaining people is not personal follow-up or joining a small group; it is being involved from the very beginning in service to others in the community. It is mobilization that equals assimilation. We actually have people who get upset with Mosaic at times and would like to leave, but they decide to stay because Mosaic is their connection to community ministry."[3]

In Erwin's book *An Unstoppable Force,* he expands on how service relates to assimilation: "A person who attends but does not begin to serve will drop out within a year. One can ponder all the research…on how to assimilate…new believers into the body of Christ, but it comes down to one simple variable. If people begin to serve, they stick."[4]

Laurie Beshore of Mariners Church puts it this way: "In our home you're just a guest and don't become family until you take out the garbage."

The Church of Irresistible Influence

Speaking to a large audience at Fellowship Bible Church's (FBC) "Church of Irresistible Influence" conference, senior pastor Robert Lewis tells of his "wake-up call" that led to his church's engagement in the Little Rock community. For years FBC was growing, but it was isolated from the needs of the community. He observed that when people first came to FBC, they bubbled over with enthusiasm. How could they not be excited? Fellowship Bible is a teaching church, and Robert and his staff are wonderful teachers. But Robert noted that after the first four or five years, people became bored with church unless they were involved in ministry. Good teaching (like good nutrition) wasn't enough. It was not until the church began to serve its community that members found their serving niche and continued to grow.

80 · The Externally Focused Church

To engage large numbers of people, FBC challenged themselves with the question "What can we do that would cause people to marvel and say, 'God is at work in a wonderful way, for no one could do these things unless God were with them'?" So for the past few years, FBC has joined more than a hundred other churches and more than five thousand volunteers in the greater Little Rock area to roll up their sleeves and serve their communities by building parks and playgrounds and refurbishing nearly fifty schools. They have renovated homes and provided school uniforms, school supplies, winter coats, and Christmas toys for hundreds of children. They began reaching out to the community through "LifeSkill" classes (on subjects such as finances, marriage, wellness, and aging) in public forums such as banks and hotel conference rooms, and they've had an impact on thousands of people. They have let their light shine in such a way that Jesus Christ is made real to the community.

Once a church makes this mental shift regarding how it lives in its community, it is only limited by its creativity in *how* it can be the salt and light it was meant to be.

Some Empirical Evidence

What if ministry to others is not just a potential avenue of growth but absolutely essential to our spiritual growth?

Dr. Howard Hendricks from Dallas Theological Seminary made this statement in reference to discipleship: "We begin to grow when we take responsibility for the growth of another person."[5] Although most Christian leaders intellectually embrace this thought, they fall back on the assumption that, given enough truth and time, their people will grow. But what if ministry to others is not just a potential avenue of growth but absolutely essential to *our* spiritual growth? What if ministry to others is really essential to our growth rather than merely incidental? What if 100 percent of Christians were ministering in some capacity inside the church or in our communities? Can we even imagine all that would change? Communities would change, churches would change, and those within the church would be changed. To find out if my assumptions about growth were true, I (Eric) conducted a ten-question survey.

The Participants—The participants were eighty-two attendees of three adult Sunday school classes from my own church—Calvary Bible Evangelical Free Church in Boulder, Colorado. Calvary Bible was established in 1889 as a mission to Swedish immigrants, so it has a long history in our community. The average weekly adult attendance is approximately 650, so my sample group of eighty-two adults is 12.6 percent of the adult worship service attendees.

For the past two years, our senior pastor, Tom Shirk, has been emphasizing involvement in ministry outside the walls of the church. Though moving at the "speed of church," we are slowly becoming an externally focused church. Within this time period, we have funded and built a Habitat for Humanity house, provided overflow housing one night a week for the homeless shelter, visited scores of families of prisoners through Prison Fellowship's Angel Tree ministry, hosted a number of bicycle tune-up clinics in low income neighborhoods, led in the refurbishing of a facility for runaway youth, refurbished four apartments at the local safe house for victims of domestic abuse, hosted a blood drive, helped begin a ministry to the homeless in partnership with another church, and launched a youth mentoring program. Other individuals are working with Sudanese "lost boys" and a myriad of community ministries. We're trying to be a church that is making a difference in our community. And we found out it's making a big difference in our own lives.

Unexpected Discoveries—Do ministry and service to others positively affect the spiritual growth of Christians? The results of my survey indicate that the answer is a resounding "yes." The following is a summary of the findings:

- **Discovery 1**—Ministry to others has a positive effect on spiritual growth. Ninety-two percent of those surveyed said that their ministry or service to others had a "positive effect" on their spiritual growth, and 8 percent said it had a "neutral effect." None said that service affected them negatively.

- **Discovery 2**—Ministry to others is almost always *as* beneficial as or *more* beneficial than other spiritual disciplines that contribute to spiritual growth. Twenty-four percent found their service to others more instrumental in their growth than any other spiritual discipline, including prayer and Bible study. Nearly all the rest said that service was as beneficial as their other spiritual disciplines in their spiritual growth.

- **Discovery 3**—People who are ministering to others are more likely to be satisfied with the level of their spiritual growth than are those who are not ministering to others. Eighty-eight percent of those who were serving were satisfied with their level of spiritual growth, while only 42 percent of those who were not serving were satisfied with their level of spiritual growth.

If the results of this survey are even close to accurate, then we are never doing people in the church a favor by encouraging them to come and just listen and take notes…if we want them to grow.

The results of this survey also quantify the experience of leaders whose people are engaged in ministry and service. Kenton Beshore, senior pastor at Mariners Church, says:

> We do nothing and give to nothing where our people are not involved. We tell our congregation, "If you give money to a ministry, then we want you to get involved in that ministry." Our biggest surprise was we knew we'd make a difference in the lives of the poor, but our involvement was better for our church than it was for them. The biggest change occurred in the life of the church. People gave of themselves, and *their* lives were changed. We often tell our people, "You need the poor and needy more than they need you." Because of this response we've had a 40 percent growth in volunteers per year.[6]

Paul writes to Philemon, "I pray that you may be active in sharing your faith, so that you will have a full understanding of every good thing we have in Christ" (Philemon 1:6). It's in outwardly sharing our faith that we gain inward understanding. Christianity is not just about helping you become a better person; Christ came into your life so you could also help make the world a better place.

> It's in outwardly sharing our faith that we gain inward understanding.

Why Do You Stand Here Idle?

Several years ago I (Eric) was in Mexico City at the Zócalo. The Zócalo is one of the largest public squares in the world, ranking right up there with Tiananmen Square in Beijing and Red Square in Moscow. On the north side of the Zócalo sits the impressive cathedral. Around the cathedral are the day laborers who sit patiently holding cardboard signs naming their occupations—"plomero" (plumber), "electricista" (electrician), "carpintero" (carpenter). There they sit, waiting to be hired. On good days they find work because local businesses often need their services. It's a very efficient picture of market forces at work—the supply and the demand are balanced quite nicely.

In the church also, there are masses of people milling around, doing nothing. And the church has jobs that need to be done. Church leaders are always looking for people to work in the nursery, teach a Sunday school class, usher or greet, sing in the choir, or serve on a board or committee. But the majority of the people standing around in the church don't have cardboard signs that say "Sunday school teacher" or "usher." They have signs that read "mechanic" or "decorator" or "equestrian," but unfortunately, in many cases, the church has no jobs for people who could use these skills as an outlet for ministry.

When the U.S. Labor Department releases the unemployment figures for the quarter, and that number is above 7 percent, it is viewed as a crisis. When a church releases its 80 percent unemployment figures (reflecting the 20 percent of "active" members), it is seen as normal. What if we were only satisfied if 100 percent of our people were engaged in some type of ministry?

What if we were only satisfied if 100 percent of our people were engaged in some type of ministry?

If your community is like ours, needs abound. And in your church are underutilized assets—people. This is one of the great inefficiencies between the church and the community, but it also provides one of our greatest opportunities. We have people with desperate needs, and we have people who long to make a difference. What if we could link them together? What if there was a way to engage the passions of 100 percent of our people in meaningful ministry?

Recently I (Eric) met with a wonderful woman in our community named Laura Kinder, the executive director of the Volunteer Connection for Boulder County. The Volunteer Connection works with hundreds of nonprofits in our county and endeavors to connect people who want to help with those organizations. She brought with her a list of three hundred organizations that she considered potential partnering opportunities for the churches of our community.

The list was alphabetized by topic, and the first topic was "animals." I glanced down the list and saw an organization called Medicine Horse that had something to do with horses. Assuming I knew what I was talking about, I commented that I really didn't think a horse clinic would be a good match for churches. Then Laura told me what this organization does. "They work with abused kids and abandoned colts. The kids feed and nurture these colts, and it's been found that this 'parenting process' is redemptive and healing in the lives of the children." Another woman who had joined us almost came out of her chair with excitement. "I grew up raising show horses, and I love kids. How can I get involved in that today?"

Given enough opportunities, everybody will find the intersection of passion and purpose.

You see, every person is born with a passion. Every person who is "born again" also has a purpose—to do the good works that God has prepared beforehand (Ephesians 2:10). Given enough opportunities, everybody will find the intersection of passion and purpose. Fulfillment is not the exclusive property of vocational Christian workers. One pastor commented, "Just when I think we've found all the willing volunteers in our church, I present another opportunity, and a whole new group comes forward." To help people grow, we need to present many opportunities for ministry.

In Matthew 20:1-16 Jesus tells the story of a landowner who went out to hire workers for his vineyard. Four times he went into the marketplace to hire day laborers. An hour before quitting time, he went out a fifth time "and found still others standing around. He asked them, 'Why have you been standing here all day long doing nothing?'

" 'Because no one has hired us,' they answered.

"He said to them, 'You also go and work in my vineyard.' "

Sometimes people are standing idle because no one has "hired" them; no one has asked them to join in this wonderful venture called *the harvest*. The landowner persists in getting laborers involved until all who can be working are working. Some have worked twelve hours, and some have worked only one hour, but ultimately all were at work in the vineyard.

Redefining Ministry

We in the church have often defined *ministry* too narrowly. In doing so, we have limited the opportunities for meaningful ministry. People long to make a difference, even if they have to go outside the church to do so. A few years ago, Calvary Bible Church in Boulder conducted a survey and discovered that their people were already serving in eighteen different human-service agencies. No one had ever thought of defining their efforts as "ministry," but that is what they were. We need to redefine *ministry*. Ministry is simply "meeting another's need with the resources God has given to you." That's enough of a definition to get us started exploring the possibilities.

Where Do We Go From Here?

If every Christian can benefit from ministry to others, then it would seem that to settle for anything less than 100 percent of Christians serving is a waste of kingdom resources of prodigal proportions. Ministry is for the mechanic as well as the minister, the teenager as well as the tenured. How can we get more people involved in ministry? The following suggestions may be helpful:

> **Ministry is for the mechanic as well as the minister, the teenager as well as the tenured.**

1. **Rediscover what the Scriptures say about good works and good deeds.** [7] At a minimum, we need to understand that each of us is God's unique creation and that each of us is created for good works. We are most likely familiar with Ephesians 2:8-9: "For it is by grace you have been saved, through faith—and this not from yourselves, it is the gift of God—not by works, so that no one can boast." We then like to put a giant period after verse 9 without reading verse 10. We should be captivated by Ephesians 2:10: "For we are God's workmanship, created in Christ Jesus to do good works, which God prepared in advance for us to do."

We are not saved *by* good works, but we are saved *for* good works that "God [has] prepared in advance for us to do." Our job is not to invent those good works but to discover what they are. How we are made (our skills and desires) is probably an indication of the type of good works we will be passionate about—where our desires and skills intersect with the needs of the world around us. It is in ministering in that intersection that we will feel most alive.

Many Christians feel empty and frustrated and go from Bible study to seminar to the latest Christian book, hoping to fill the "purpose void" with more personal development or insight. It is more likely that until we discover our place of ministry, we will not feel the satisfaction of Ephesians 2:10—doing the good works God has prepared in advance for us to do. In a recent Bible study, after carefully studying the Ephesians 2:8-10 passage, one man blurted out, "If I'm his workmanship, and he's prepared good works for *me*, well, that means that *my* good works don't have to look like *your* good works!"

> **The way to inwardly build a church is through outward service.**

The church also is strengthened as its people engage in good works. The way to *inwardly* build a church is through *outward* service. God gives gifted leaders to the church "to prepare God's people for works of service, so that the body of Christ may be built up" (Ephesians 4:12). There can be no "building up" until people are engaged in works of service. God saved us to do good works; church leadership is there to prepare people for good works; the Word of God equips us "for every good work" (from 2 Timothy 3:17), and we are to "spur one another on toward love and good deeds" (Hebrews 10:24). Now the question is: Will we follow through by actually engaging in good works?

There is a vast difference between bodybuilding and weight training. If you've ever been channel-surfing and caught a bodybuilding contest on ESPN, you know that the purpose of bodybuilding is to maximally develop every muscle in the human body and then, with the help of a good tan, a small bathing suit, shiny skin, and striking poses, to show it off. But to what end? For what purpose? There is no end; there is no purpose beyond building up the body! That's it. Weight training is different. Athletic records are continually being shattered largely because the strength and capacity of athletes are increasing through weight training. For athletes, weight training is a means to a greater end. Strength, flexibility, and speed are their goal—not the size of their muscles. These athletes train *for* their event. Their training is not the event.

The purpose of the church should be more than "body" building. The church should be more like a training facility designed to equip the saints for works of service.

This is the criterion for effectiveness that Lighthouse Ministries of Mariners Church in Irvine, California, has adopted: "We continually evaluate our work based on the life change experienced by our volunteers and those we serve in our community." That's a great start in building a virtuous cycle of ministry. If ministry does something for the people you are serving but nothing for you, it will be difficult to sustain. If ministry does something for you but nothing for them…well, that doesn't work either. It's only when *all* benefit that ministries will be sustainable.

2. Broaden the definition of *ministry*. Most Christians have been conditioned to think of ministry as something that professional ministers do or missionaries report about. In a church setting, service is usually limited to the "sacred seven"—working in the nursery, teaching a Sunday school class, leading a home group, singing on the worship team, ushering, greeting, or serving on a board or committee. But ministry is so much more than that.

> **We don't do our people any favors by letting them attend church every week, living with the illusion that they are growing. They may be learning, but they are not growing.**

Ministry, again, is "meeting another's needs with the resources God gives to you." Yes, ministry is preaching the gospel and discipling others, but it is also binding up the brokenhearted and comforting those who mourn (Isaiah 61:1, 2). It is "[sharing] your food with the hungry and [providing] the poor wanderer with shelter" (Isaiah 58:7a). Ministry is being "merciful, just as your Father is merciful" (Luke 6:36).

Who defines *ministry* in your church? Most likely it is the pastor. If you are the senior pastor of your church, you are in a unique position to define ministry there and to bless and commission people in these ministries. Many people are ready, willing, and awaiting your commissioning.

3. Present "ministry to others" as part and parcel of the normal Christian life. Set the bar high. Determine that every Christian in your church will minister to others in some capacity. (Even engaging non-Christians in service to others is often their avenue to personal salvation.) We don't do our people any favors by letting them attend church every week, living with the illusion that they are growing. They may be learning, but they are not growing.

James 1:22 says, "Do not merely listen to the word, and so deceive yourselves. Do what it says." James goes on to say, "Faith by itself, if it is not accompanied by action, is dead" (James 2:17). All Christians may not be Bible scholars or evangelists, but all Christians, regardless of their present level of maturity, can meet someone else's need with the resources God has given them. The good Samaritan was not a theologian—remember that the theologians in the story were too busy—but he demonstrated mercy in alleviating suffering and providing care and companionship to one in need. We meet Jesus through service (Matthew 25:40) and are never more like Jesus than when we are serving others (John 13:13-15).

Can everybody really do ministry? Sometimes people want to come to your church because they need to heal and rest. Everything in them tells them that they just need to be ministered to. They have absolutely nothing to give. There may be seasons when this is appropriate, but remember the Lord's words spoken through Isaiah (58:7-8a): "Is it not to share your food with the hungry and to provide the poor wanderer with shelter—when you see the naked, to clothe him, and not to turn away from your own flesh and blood? Then your light will break forth like the dawn, and your healing will quickly appear." It is in ministering to others that we ourselves are healed.

> **It is in ministering to others that we ourselves are healed.**

Physical therapy is painful. When our bodies are screaming, "Just lie there! Don't move a muscle," it is the doctor who gets us up and exercising, knowing that in our exercise, not just in our rest, we are healed. The church is a place of rehabilitation, not convalescence. It is not a hospice that prepares people to die; it is a rehab center preparing people to live.

Wouldn't it be great if on any given Sunday you could point randomly to any person in your congregation and say, "Please tell us about your ministry," and every person that was called upon would come forth with a description of how God is using him or her in ministry to others? Some people might minister a couple of days a year, building a Habitat for Humanity house. Others might minister weekly to migrant workers. But everybody would be doing something. Doing nothing is the only unacceptable option.

Remembering the Grinch

How the Grinch Stole Christmas has a happy ending because, in the end, Grinch's heart "grew three sizes that day." His capacity to love and to feel compassion grew. Jesus is in the process of enlarging the size of our hearts, increasing our capacity to love. Expanding our capacity to love was the lesson he taught his disciples in Luke 6:27-32: "Love...do good...bless...pray for..." and "If you love those who love you, what credit is that to you?"

We will naturally love those to whom by affinity or affection we are attracted. Jesus asks his followers to go beyond that type of love. In John 21:15-18, when Jesus asked Peter three times, "Do you love me?" he was asking Peter to expand his capacity to love. Jack Jezreel of JustFaith (www.justfaith.org) says, "Everything is in service to this—expanding the size of our hearts. People with small brains and big hearts can accomplish great things."[8] Zacchaeus' heart grew the day he met Jesus. What was once encased with greed softened and grew. He was transformed from a thief to a philanthropist.

The test of your spiritual growth is simple—How has your heart grown in the past twelve months? Are your arms open wider toward others, or are they wrapped around yourself? Do you have room for anyone else in your life? An acquaintance pondered this question and said to me, "You know, when I first became a Christian, I had a really small house but a really big heart. Now I have a really big house but a really small heart. I want a bigger heart." Some of us might be Grinches by nature—born to be takers and not givers. But at some point, we've got to allow the Lord to grow us up and change and expand our hearts. It's just not OK to remain a Grinch.

Something to **Think** About

Lighthouse Ministries' criterion for effectiveness: "Our success is defined by life change. We continually evaluate our work based on the life change experienced by our volunteers and those we serve in our community. Our greatest reward is seeing God's transforming work in all of our lives as we serve Him." We often tell our people, "You need the poor and needy more than they need you."

Something to **Talk** About

1. How have your ministry and service toward others helped you grow and experience God?

2. How has your heart grown in the past twelve months?

Something to **Act** Upon

1. What steps could you take to engage 100 percent of your church members in some type of ministry or service to others?

2. What specific steps will you take to identify the needs and dreams of your community?

3. Where are the areas of "low-hanging fruit" where those in your church could begin serving?

Sermon/**Lesson** Idea

Text: Ephesians 2:8-10

Main Idea: Ephesians 2:8-9 clearly explains that we are saved and made right with God by grace through faith alone...apart from any work. Salvation is God's unmerited gift to us. Ephesians 2:10 completes the passage: We are his workmanship, created *for* good works. Good works don't save us, but we are saved for good works.

Illustration: Survey results (see pages 82-83), the importance of both diet and exercise

Action Point: Set a goal for increasing the percentage of people in your church who are serving and ministering.

Endnotes

1. Kirbyjon Caldwell, foreword to *The Equipping Church* by Sue Mallory (Grand Rapids, MI: Zondervan, 2001), 9.

2. Terry Anderson, comments (Phoenix, AZ: conversation with Eric Swanson, June 6, 2003).

3. Erwin Raphael McManus, comments (conversation with Eric Swanson, May 22, 2001).

4. Erwin Raphael McManus, *An Unstoppable Force* (Loveland, CO: Group Publishing, Inc, 2001), 174.

5. Howard Hendricks (Fort Collins, CO: series of lectures given at Colorado State University, July 1978).

6. Kenton Beshore, comments (Dallas, TX: Leadership Network's Wild Challenge, May 28, 2003).

7. See especially 1 Timothy 2:9-10; 1 Timothy 6:18; Titus 2:7, 14; Hebrews 10:24; 1 Peter 2:12. See also other references beginning on page 219 of the Appendix.

8. Jack Jezreel, comments (Boulder, CO: lecture given at Sacred Heart of Jesus Church, December 16, 2002).

chapter five

Nothing **Happens** Outside of **Relationships**

"The first responsibility of a leader is to define reality. The last is to say thank you. In between the two, the leader must become a servant."

—Max De Pree [1]

Failing to Relate

Dun and Bradstreet conducted a study to determine why executives fail. The organization studied twelve hundred executives who had been fired from their jobs. Interestingly, it wasn't their market expertise, financial understanding, or product knowledge that was the primary cause for failure. In 85 percent of the cases, their relational skills were the cause.[2] The same might be true of churches. If we were to study the primary reason churches fail, we might discover that they've failed in the one area they should be good at—building, sustaining, and cultivating relationships.

The Church Grows Through Relationships

In the early centuries of the church, Christ's followers, through their compassion and kindness, served the people around them. As a result, it is estimated that the early church grew at a rate of 40 percent per decade during its first several centuries.[3] The early Christians didn't have direct mail, large special events, or banners to get their message across. All they had were themselves. "They followed a daily discipline of worship in the Temple followed by meals at home, every meal a celebration, exuberant and joyful, as they praised God. People in general liked what they saw. Every day their number grew as God added those who were saved" (Acts 2:46-47, *The Message*). God entrusted his message to the church then, and that responsibility is still ours today. While events can help us gather the masses, they can't take the place of Christians rubbing shoulders with non-Christians.

The church that develops long-term, trusting relationships with the community is the one that has an opportunity to influence its culture. The most effective way to do that seems to be in the context of serving. In meeting the needs of others and serving alongside them, we cannot help but create relationship. Relationship is key to building bridges into the community.

A Closer Look

Rubbing Shoulders

Gary was the pastor of a small church in Indiana. When he first moved into the small farming community, he found an innovative way to get to know his new surroundings. He joined the volunteer fire department. Through this simple act of civil service, great relationships were formed.

The volunteer fire department in that small town was made up of several young men. These men had little or no interest in church. Many of them had visited the local church as children, but as adults they didn't return to church on their own. Through building friendships with the men during their hours of serving the community together, the young pastor began to understand their hesitancy to revisit church.

One day, one of the young firefighters said to Gary, "Well, I'd go to church, but I don't have a suit." This may sound like a lame excuse, but Gary realized it was more than that. That young firefighter was serious. When Gary told the group that wearing a suit certainly isn't required or even expected, these down-to-earth guys were surprised. Since as adults they had only set foot in a church to attend weddings and funerals, they didn't realize that many men no longer wear suits at worship services.

Many of those men have now come back to the small church, brought their families, and entered into the kingdom because of Gary's willingness to eat meals with them, fight fires with them, and serve with them. This young pastor found a way to enter into authentic relationships in his community.

As we discussed in earlier chapters, many externally focused churches have made inroads into their communities by partnering with other organizations that are meeting community needs. Churches have had both success and failure in these partnerships. Over the years, some basic relationship-building principles have become apparent.

Recognize That Relationships Take Time

Building long-term, trusting relationships with the community doesn't happen overnight. When the people of LifeBridge Christian Church first began A Time to Serve, we met with resistance from a few leaders of local nonprofit agencies. Our offer of hundreds of volunteers for only short periods of time didn't always work for the people we were trying to help. Some nonprofits didn't have the organizational structure in place to handle many volunteers, and they needed plenty of lead time to make it work. Some wondered if the church could really pull it off. They even questioned whether the volunteers from LifeBridge would really show up. They didn't want to put all of their eggs in one basket, and this was understandable.

It took a lot of phone calls, meetings, and prayer to get through the first year of A Time to Serve. But because people worked very hard to fulfill their volunteer commitments during that first year, the second year was a little smoother. Rapport had been created.

As we began preparations for year three of A Time to Serve, the excitement was palpable. As early as July, local nonprofits started calling the church office, asking to be included in our list of projects. Many nonprofits in the Longmont community now look forward to working alongside LifeBridge volunteers, and they work with us to plan special projects. They call the church throughout the year, not just at Christmastime. Relationships have been built, and trust has been established.

Finish What You Start

It is said that a reporter once asked Henry Ford what makes for a successful life, and he responded, "Always finish what you start." I don't know if Ford actually said this, but I do know he lived it. Getting started is often the biggest problem we face, but finishing requires perseverance and determination over the long haul.

Sometimes churches have bitten off more than they could chew, and LifeBridge is no exception. In our case, the result was mutual disappointment in the partnership. Since then, we've learned some important lessons. First, make sure that the church and the community organization both clearly understand each other's needs and expectations. Second, begin slowly, if possible. Third, ensure that one person with passion for the project is responsible for it. (This must be true on both ends of the partnership.) Finally, no matter what hurdles you face along the way, remain committed to finishing what you start!

A Closer Look

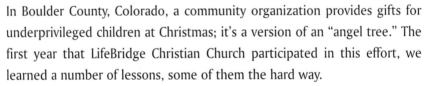

Too Many Angels!

In Boulder County, Colorado, a community organization provides gifts for underprivileged children at Christmas; it's a version of an "angel tree." The first year that LifeBridge Christian Church participated in this effort, we learned a number of lessons, some of them the hard way.

First, the lines of communication weren't clear. The result was misunderstandings about who was providing what. For example, the county volunteer coordinator thought we had committed to providing volunteers for the distribution effort. At LifeBridge, we had either missed that information or misunderstood what we were expected to do. When the day for sorting and delivery came, the twenty-five volunteers expected from LifeBridge didn't show. More than a few people were hot under the collar at our lack of helping.

In addition, we overestimated our ability to get the job done. We thought our congregation of nine hundred (at that time) could easily help the thousand children in the program. While our obligations to these children were eventually met, plenty of scrambling, some confusion, and a whole lot of arm-twisting were required to get the job done. Once again, the organizers saw us as bumbling our way through.

Finally, we hadn't yet learned how to help the people of LifeBridge celebrate their efforts. We didn't share any personal stories, take any pictures, or offer opportunities for personal participation with the children, beyond buying gifts. We work hard to avoid these kinds of mistakes today.

Fortunately, the county project coordinators were gracious enough to see beyond our poor first effort. In the intervening years, LifeBridge has become an integral part of this community effort, and now we are entrusted with a thousand angels without hesitation!

Partner With Any Organization That Is Morally Positive and Spiritually Neutral

Every community is blessed with people who genuinely care about its health and welfare. They express their concern in countless ways and are involved in pressing issues such as homelessness, addictions, children, the elderly, parks, clean streets, and safer neighborhoods. The opportunities for the church to come alongside those who are addressing these needs are endless. Even though we may attribute different causes to the problems, identify different solutions, and ultimately have different perspectives on humanity, we can work together with community organizations in the common cause of bettering the community. At times, this may lead to a connection with organizations that churches wouldn't normally support or assist.

Should churches assist local community agencies with which they don't always agree? This tough question has often led Christians to provide alternative versions of the same services. But more and more churches are now willing to partner with groups whose views they don't share. Instead of getting hung up on the issues, they look for common ground to meet the needs Jesus outlines in Matthew 25:35-36: "For I was hungry and you gave me something to eat, I was thirsty and you gave me something to drink, I was a stranger and you invited me in, I needed clothes and you clothed me, I was sick and you looked after me, I was in prison and you came to visit me."

If churches can honor God through serving the needs of the community and creating relationships with those leading the local agencies; we may have the opportunity to share the good news of God's grace. Maybe the people who disagree with us will ultimately choose Christ, maybe they will learn his ways, and maybe they will change some of the policies and philosophies that do not honor God. Maybe someday the people who govern our cities, lead our schools, and oversee our community agencies will be people of faith who seek to honor God through their work.

A Closer Look

When Partners Don't See Eye to Eye

(Because of the sensitive nature of this story, the church, the community organization, and the city will remain unnamed.)

A local crisis center needed volunteers. The center assisted women and children who had been abused or were in significant financial need. Many of the women were single moms struggling to provide for their children. Several members of a local church already volunteered their time at this shelter; through their involvement, the church was asked to provide clothing, food, limited financial assistance, and maintenance help.

The shelter's director was a wonderful woman whose compassion for the people she served was evident. Early in the church's relationship with this organization, however, the director made it clear that she had no interest in "religion" and didn't want the church pushing its views on anybody. In fact, she made it clear that the only reason the church was involved was because the organization needed the help and church members were already connected to the work.

One of the services the shelter provided was counseling. The director was adamant that any woman who was pregnant and at the shelter should get an abortion. She was convinced that bringing another child into the situation was unwarranted. In addition, the shelter would provide the necessary funds to pay for the abortion.

Needless to say, this put the church in a bind. How could the church provide assistance in the face of this totally unacceptable approach? Church members met with the director to discuss their concerns and their church's position on abortion. They also asked the director for a solution to the dilemma, instead of closing the door on helping the shelter. The director remained adamant that her approach to these pregnancies would not change.

At the time, it seemed that the church should just find another place that needed the help. However, this was an important community need, and people in the church were already passionate about the shelter. The solution? The church agreed to find ways to help the shelter's battered women, and the director agreed that no resources from the church would be given to assist women with abortion.

This may not have been an ideal solution, but the story is not finished yet. What happened after that was more interesting. As the church volunteers gained credibility, more opportunities for involvement occurred. The church was invited to find volunteers to provide mentoring, job training, and child care. It was a wonderful opportunity to build relationships that might affect the eternity of the women in the shelter.

It would be nice to be able to say that through the gracious service and witness of Christians, the director changed her viewpoint and, even better, gave her life to Christ. That didn't happen. What did happen? Eventually she moved out of the state to pursue another opportunity. In the search for her replacement, a number of the church volunteers were invited to be part of the interviewing process. Guess what view the new director doesn't hold.

Recognize That Conflict Is Inevitable

We may not always agree with other community service groups on the cause or cure, but we do agree there is a problem. Understand that conflict will arise, but begin the relationship at that place of agreement. The best way to resolve conflict is to have had some basis for relationship. The stronger the relational bond, the more significant the conflict will have to be in order to break or severely damage the relationship. With people I (Rick) don't know well, it doesn't take much to cause me to back away at even the slightest conflict. But the deeper my investment in the relationship, the stronger my desire to resolve the conflict.

We tend to think that a relationship can be successful only if every issue that arises between the two parties is resolved. In reality, though, relationships rarely work that way. In my marriage to Diane, for example, we haven't always agreed on resolutions to conflicts. We have, however, decided that reconciliation can happen even when resolution does not. We've learned that "we can walk hand in hand when we don't see eye to eye."

> **Reconciliation can happen even when resolution does not.**

When conflict occurs and we reach an impasse, Diane and I have to back up to our point of agreement. Not long ago we had completely different approaches to handling a parenting issue. We had hit an impasse. No amount of discussing, passion, or strong-arming was going to move either one of us. So we backed up until we found common ground. We agreed that there was a problem. We agreed on the causes. We agreed that it would be irresponsible to do nothing. We agreed that we loved our child. From there, we moved toward our areas of disagreement. Finally we decided to take an approach that one of us didn't think was the best solution, give it a chance, and see how things turned out. We didn't agree on the resolution, but we agreed on the relationship, so we were able to move forward.

If what matters is creating and sustaining relationships with other community groups, we must start with the areas on which we agree—and build from there.

Recently I had a conversation with a public official about some of the issues facing our community and ways the church might help. This person's views were the opposite of mine. The person doesn't share my faith perspective and, in fact, isn't interested in faith of any kind. We don't share the same political views. We aren't even close in our views on how to address community problems.

We do agree that there are some problems and that they need to be addressed or they will create more significant ones. With that as a starting point, we began to discuss ways the church could help. During the course of the conversation, we frequently had to return to the point on which we agreed, but eventually the conversation moved in a positive direction. We identified further areas of agreement; we initiated small steps of mutual participation. Credibility was established, and the relationship deepened. This has led to further involvement between the community organization and the church.

Develop Partnerships
With No Strings Attached

One rule of thumb is that churches should come only to serve and bless, not to control. When we partner or aid an organization in our community, we understand that sometimes the church is merely the hands and feet, not the mouth and brain, of the project. Respect the position and the passion of the people with whom you are trying to partner.

Proverbs 27:17 says, "As iron sharpens iron, so one man sharpens another." As you brainstorm with community organizations, be open to learning from their leadership. In many cases, they may have been studying and working on the issue at hand much longer than the people in your church. Their motivation for serving may not be the same as yours, but resolution and mutual respect are still possible and necessary.

> **Always ask the organizations in your community, "How can we help you?" and don't worry about who gets the credit.**

Always ask the organizations in your community, "How can we help you?" and don't worry about who gets the credit. I know it's hard not to keep score: "We did that. Our people helped there. That happened because our church was involved." That sort of scorekeeping doesn't promote or sustain healthy, bridge-building relationships.

People respond well when you put their needs above your own. Paul challenges us to do just that in Philippians 2:3-4: "Do nothing out of selfish ambition or vain conceit, but in humility consider others better than yourselves. Each of you should look not only to your own interests, but also to the interests of others." I love *The Message's* version of this verse: "Don't be obsessed with getting your own advantage. Forget yourselves long enough to lend a helping hand."

A Closer Look

Is There Anything We Can Do for You?

Flatirons Community Church is a vibrant church that is experiencing explosive growth in a small town outside of Boulder, Colorado. After outgrowing their storefront location and moving into a renovated box store, they wanted to make a deeper connection with the community. Senior Pastor Gil Jones and two associates made an appointment with the mayor and asked, "Is there anything we can do for you?"

The mayor responded, "Do you like helping kids?"

Speaking for the church, Gil responded, "That's right up our alley!"

So the mayor told them about an elementary school that was in sad shape. Sixty percent of the students are classified as poor. Seventy-five percent come from broken families, and 50 percent consider a language other than English as their primary language. Many of the kids' test scores showed that they were performing at two full grade levels below their ages. The school was nothing less than a miracle waiting to happen.

The church's offer to help came with no strings attached, and it was agreed not to use "Jesus speak" with the faculty or students. Even so, the school's response was not exactly overwhelming. Volunteers were asked to barcode books for the library, and a few teachers requested help with children with special needs. Rather than feeling slighted, the volunteers did an extraordinary thing: They showed up…day after day, week after week…and they did whatever was asked of them. Within three months something wonderful happened. Jesus began to speak through their acts of kindness and love. Now, when volunteers walk into a classroom, children come running with smiles and open arms.

Recently this school was one of a handful to receive a $500,000 grant based on its ability to effectively use volunteers. During the evaluation, when asked how the school would effectively recruit and utilize volunteers, the principal responded, "We have all the help we need from Flatirons. They've been amazing. I'm confident that they will take care of whatever needs we have."[4]

Promote and Practice Gracious Evangelism

You usually won't find LifeBridge Christian Church volunteers wearing T-shirts screaming their church's mission statement or volunteers singing "Amazing Grace" as they serve lunch at the soup kitchen. As your church builds relational bridges, watch for opportunities to share God's grace, but don't force the message. Over time, people will be intrigued by your serving and will probe, ask questions, and invite you to share your individual stories of what Jesus has done for you.

I was once asked by a church in our area if some of its members could assist us with a community project. We were glad to have them. The person they'd appointed to lead this effort wanted to know when in the day we were going to stop and share the gospel message with the group we were serving. Assuming he meant have a pointed lesson in which we announced who we were and what we believed, I told him we weren't there to do that. Then he asked if they could wear their hats and shirts with their logos on them so people knew who was helping. You can guess my answer. We decided long ago that we aren't going to serve to get noticed. We serve for two reasons: to meet basic needs and to create positive relationships.

One of the best illustrations of gracious evangelism is Penny's story. Penny first became familiar with LifeBridge because she works at one of the community-service agencies with which we partner. Penny saw firsthand that the volunteers from LifeBridge care about the community, and it made an impression on her. Penny is now a committed Christian who serves in the church and the community as the director of a nonprofit organization in Longmont. No one gave her a tract or twisted her arm to come to church. She was led to Christ by what she saw, not by what she was told.

Tear Down Old Assumptions

Over the years, I've discovered that, for the most part, people in leadership positions in our community genuinely desire to make the community a better place. Certainly there are those who do what they do for personal gain or because it's just a job or a steppingstone to something better. (I know of ministry folks who could fall in this category!) But in general, individuals charged with responsibility for the community have the community's interests at heart.

In connecting with these people, I have experienced two responses that have caught me off guard. First, the non-Christians among them haven't had very positive things to say about how the Christians in the community voice their concerns. For example, one school administrator told me that most of his experiences with Christian parents have been hostile. He said that if Christian parents don't like something about the school system, rather than discussing it or looking for solutions, they simply blast the system with diatribes about the school's lack of character, morality, and so on. This school administrator admitted that though the parents often had good reasons for concern, their demeanor put them in the position of adversaries. (Please note that he also told me of Christian parents who responded with grace and often got good results. But according to this school district employee, this didn't seem to be the majority approach.)

I have heard stories about Christians behaving badly too many times, in too many settings, not to be convinced that there is some truth to them. In fairness, many community officials are predisposed against Christians, so they tend to exaggerate their flaws.

The second response that caught me off guard was that nearly every time our church has offered to help in the community, community leaders initially didn't see how we could be of any real help. Often they would say, "If there is a need for spiritual counseling, we'll let you know. If people are looking for 'religious help,' we'll send them your way." Other than that, they wondered how the church could possibly be of any help to their organization.

There is no question that the church has been marginalized in our society. However it has happened, the church is seen, in George Barna's words, as an "island of piety, surrounded by a sea of irrelevance."[5] We could debate the hows and whys all day long, but the fact remains that the church is generally not viewed as an important part of the fabric of the community. In most places the church has lost any voice on the issues and needs facing the community. The church isn't on the list of resources community leaders consult when looking for assistance in resolving the challenges they face.

A Closer Look

"I Just Didn't Think the Church Would Help."

He had relocated to Colorado to become the principal of one of the troubled elementary schools in our town. This school had low test scores and poor attendance. It was on the watch list. His first year was a marked success. Test scores improved; attendance rates increased; teacher morale and parental involvement grew. His second year allowed him to move from the "emergency room" to "long-term care." He discovered a number of systemic issues related to language barriers, mobility, and the basic financial needs of the students and their families. One day on his way to a meeting, he pulled into the LifeBridge Christian Church parking lot, hesitated to come in, and nearly changed his mind. Then he got out of his car and came in, hoping to catch me there.

He told me why he had given up a successful position with the state's Department of Education and moved to Boulder. Then he continued, "I have been in town for a year, and I've been told by some of our teachers and staff that LifeBridge would be a place to get help."

He continued, "I'm not sure I should ask, but I've thought of four different ways I think the church could help." What an opportunity! His needs were related to mentoring, tutoring, ESL (English as a Second Language), and the need for coats and books. He also indicated that he thought the students' parents would be interested in connecting with us if we were interested.

"We'd be honored to be a part of what you're trying to accomplish," I said.

I was surprised by what he said next: "You won't believe how nervous I was about stopping here."

"How come?" I asked.

"My dad was a minister and a really good man, but I just didn't think the church would help this way, and I hated to ask."

After our meeting, I was left with two impressions. First, this principal had come because people around him had heard of or had experience with people from LifeBridge—relationship.

Second, even though he had grown up in a Christian environment, he was surprised to find a church eager to offer practical assistance to the community.

Make It Personal

After learning that community leaders generally don't trust Christians and that the church doesn't have a reputation for being very helpful, I became more passionate about finding ways to engage the community and discovering paths that might lead to meaningful dialogue. I wanted people in our community, when they were in need, to think of the church first.

As a church, LifeBridge approached these issues pragmatically. We didn't conduct studies, hold a popular vote, or emulate other churches' methods. We simply decided that nothing in the world happens outside of relationships…and that the best way to create relationships is to enter the world of those you seek to know, rather than waiting for them to enter yours.

We learned that the best way for our church to engage the community was to discover ways to be useful. That has meant that each of us—every staff person, every leader, and every member—is personally challenged to make a connection with the community through serving.

> **As the senior minister, I have been challenged to do more than just talk about all of this.**

As the senior minister, I have been challenged to do more than just talk about all of this. The problem of underage drinking made the front page of the local newspaper. In response, a school official put together a small task force to discuss what could be done. This task force initially included the mayor, the police chief, the assistant superintendent of the school district, a principal, and me. I was asked because the school official knew me from other community events and realized that, since I had two teenagers at the time, I had a vested interest in the problem. This task force met every week for over a year and grew to include health officials, members of the city youth council, and business leaders. Out of these efforts came a number of community initiatives that have had moderate success in raising the awareness of underage drinking and creating a network of agencies to address the issue.

There was a time when I would have suggested the name of a staff member or a key volunteer rather than agreeing to join this task force. There was a time when I would have made all kinds of excuses for not taking on the assignments that rose out of the task force. There were certainly times when the things we were doing on the task force didn't seem to have any connection to the church at all. However, in a way I didn't realize at the time, my participation helped to establish the church's credibility in the community and gave us a stronger voice there. Because of the relationships that were created in the task force, the church has been given more opportunities to be involved.

In today's pluralistic world, with a thousand voices competing for viability and the growing pressure for tolerance among community leaders, it's more likely than ever that the church will become increasingly marginalized. Left to the current state of affairs, the gap between church and society will only widen. To me, this presents a wonderful opportunity for the church to show up with a basin and towel. In the midst of serving, we can listen and connect, and ultimately we can be heard.

The goal of an externally focused church is to serve, but the ultimate goal is to build the kingdom. This is service with a higher calling and a stronger motivation. Relationships are not only essential for gaining trust within the community; they are the door by which many individuals come into a relationship with Christ.

A Closer Look

Jack's Story
(by Jack Hay, LifeBridge Christian Church)

My wife and I had been discussing going to church for some time, but we'd done nothing about it. Eventually I suggested that we try LifeBridge. Why? Because I had developed a relationship with the senior minister, Rick Rusaw. I first met Rick at a community task force meeting designed to solve the problem of underage drinking in our community. The group met at LifeBridge and included this minister, the mayor, the police chief, health department officials, and me—an assistant superintendent in the school district. At first I didn't realize that Rick was a minister. All I knew was that he was a parent and a representative from the church. I had some preconceived notions about Christians, but my interaction with Rick broke these stereotypes. I found that he was intensely interested in finding real solutions. He wasn't what I expected.

During the time we served together on this task force, I began to realize that LifeBridge had been offering its people and facilities to our community in many large and small ways. I could see that these people were making a difference. As a school district employee and a community volunteer, I had worked to make the community better, but I found myself wanting to be a part of a bigger plan. I was attracted to LifeBridge because the people had invested themselves in my town. I was drawn to them.

My faith has continued to grow and mature. I've been involved in Bible studies, prayer events, and even a mission trip to Thailand. Now I'm focused on volunteer work to enhance community outreach. My motivation is ministry. As an educator for over thirty years, I thought my life had great purpose, but working on behalf of the kingdom has taught me what *purpose* really is!

Our goal at LifeBridge is to get people into the community, into the church, and into heaven. It's a circle of unending influence. If the pattern is repeated again and again, externally focused churches can build the kingdom throughout the world.

Something to **Think** About

"I just didn't think the church would help…"

Something to **Talk** About

1. Would the people in your community think to ask your church for help?
2. Have you ever asked your community's leaders, "How can we help you?"
3. Are you personally involved in community concerns?

Something to **Act** Upon

Assess the ways people in your church are rubbing shoulders with non-Christians. Dream up ways to meet community leaders, and take the initiative to set up the meeting.

Sermon/**Lesson** Idea

Text: 1 Corinthians 12:12-26

Main Idea:-The church won't survive with the mentality that it doesn't need the community. We need the community, and the community needs us. We need to be connected to each other for encouragement, accountability, and strength. We want the church to be

- a place where everyone makes a difference,
- a place where no one stands alone, and
- a place where authentic relationships are experienced.

Illustration: A cord of three strands is not quickly torn apart.

Action Point: Brainstorm practical new ways for the church to connect with the community through authentic relationships.

Endnotes

1. Max De Pree, *Leadership Is an Art* (New York: Dell Publishing, 1989), 11.

2. Dun and Bradstreet, "Sharpening Your People Skills," a seminar sponsored by Leadership Dynamics International, Atlanta, GA, 1991.

3. Rodney Stark, *The Rise of Christianity* (San Francisco: HarperCollins Publishers, 1996), 6.

4. John Zisch (associate pastor of Flatirons Community Church), comments (telephone conversation with Eric Swanson, May 27, 2003).

5. George Barna, comments (Cincinnati, OH: New Church Planting Conference, March 1988).

chapter six

Good **News** and Good **Deeds**

"I know this now. Every man gives his life for what he believes. Every woman gives her life for what she believes. Sometimes people believe in little or nothing yet they give their lives to that little or nothing. One life is all we have and we live it as we believe in living it. And then it is gone. But to sacrifice what you are and live without belief, that's more terrible than dying."

—Joan of Arc [1]

Josiah—An Epitaph to Remember

What will you be remembered for? What will your church be remembered for? Few of us will have biographers (praise God!) to record our foibles and successes. People usually associate great men and women with one great ideal, invention, achievement, or cause. Mention the name Lincoln, and most people will say, "freed the slaves" or "preserved the union." Mention George Washington and you'll hear, "father of our country." Martin Luther King Jr. is remembered for his "I Have a Dream" speech.

King Josiah had a couple of biographers. The writers of 2 Kings and 2 Chronicles record that he became king at the age of eight, began seeking the Lord at sixteen, rediscovered the Scriptures, and brought about spiritual and moral reforms in Judah. But the one thing that went forward from his life was the epitaph written by his contemporary, Jeremiah. The author of 2 Chronicles wrote: "Jeremiah composed laments for Josiah, and to this day all the men and women singers commemorate Josiah in the laments" (2 Chronicles 35:25a). And what was it Jeremiah wrote about Josiah? Not much really. Just a short couplet—

" 'He did what was right and just, so all went well with him. He defended the cause of the poor and needy, and so all went well. Is that not what it means to know me?' declares the Lord" (Jeremiah 22:15b-16).

Thirty-nine words have rarely been freighted with such content. To defend the cause of the poor and needy is what it means to know the Lord. It is the equation that matters. One day you'll be gone, but those who knew you will think of something when your name comes up. What will go forward from your life?

Good works are coupled with good news throughout Scripture. When summing up the ministry of Jesus, Peter simply said, "God...[told] the good news...through Jesus Christ...and...he went around doing good...because God was with him" (Acts 10:36-38). Good news and accompanying good deeds are like the two wings of an airplane. Each is incomplete without the other. Each complements the other. Each gives "lift" to the other. To study the life and ministry of Jesus is to study a tapestry woven of good news and

> **The good deeds paved the road over which his good news traveled.**

good deeds. Woven throughout the fabric of his life was a ministry of Show and Tell—of good works and good news, side by side, working powerfully together (Matthew 4:23; 9:35; Luke 4:32-37). When Jesus sent forth his disciples, "he sent them out to preach the kingdom of God and to heal the sick" (Luke 9:2). The good deeds paved the road over which his good news traveled. Every church that seeks to be more externally focused can do so with the assurance that Jesus has gone before. He has shown the way.

To follow Jesus as his disciple was to be one who engaged in good news and good deeds. One was to "be merciful, just as [God] is merciful" (Luke 6:36), love as Jesus loved (John 13:34-35), and be a neighbor to all in need (Luke 10:29-37). Jesus encouraged his followers to "let your light shine before men, that they may see your good deeds and praise your Father in heaven" (Matthew 5:16).

In Galatians 2 the Apostle Paul writes about dividing up ministry responsibilities among Peter, James, John, and himself. Paul writes, "They agreed that we should go to the Gentiles, and they to the Jews. All they asked was that we should continue to remember the poor, the very thing I was eager to do" (Galatians 2:9b-10). The word *eager* is a lot like the word *passion*. Just as one cannot be passionate about everything (or you'll be perceived as some kind of nut), one also can't be eager about everything. What comes to mind was the other thing Paul was eager to do: "I am so eager to preach the gospel also to you who are at Rome" (Romans 1:15). Of all the things Paul did, he was really eager to do only two things—preach the gospel (Acts 26:28-29) and remember the poor (Acts 24:17). He didn't need to compromise or sacrifice one to accomplish the other. He was eager to do both. He engaged in both.

How the Gospel Grew

If we can learn anything from the history of the early church, we can learn that a church without seminaries, church-growth seminars, elaborate youth programs, or large campuses can still grow at a phenomenal rate. Many sociological, political, and spiritual factors contributed to the spread of the gospel. The first century was indeed a "fullness of time" (Galatians 4:4, KJV) moment for Jesus to enter the world. One cannot deny the importance of such unprecedented conditions as a common language, the Pax Romana, and safety of travel. But in addition to these factors, the early Christians lived in such a way that caused the world to stand up and take notice, for they had a distinctive lifestyle that could not be ignored. They were followers of Christ, and as such, they sought to live as he lived, love as he loved, and if the ultimate price was to be paid, they would be welcomed into the company of Jesus himself and those who had gone before. Early Christians were captivated by the gospel and profoundly influenced by the teachings and values of Jesus Christ. We can assume from their actions that they were changed by Jesus and consumed with the values of the kingdom of God. They were more than salt and light in their communities; they were the "soul" of their communities.

If we can learn anything from the history of the early church, we can learn that a church without seminaries, church-growth seminars, elaborate youth programs, or large campuses can still grow at a phenomenal rate.

The Church With Its Sleeves Rolled Up

When the devastating plagues of the first three centuries swept over Europe, those who were able fled the cities—but not the Christians. They stayed and ministered to the sick and dying, whether they were Christians or not. Dionysius, bishop of Alexandria, described how believers responded to the plague of 260:

> The most of our brethren were unsparing in their exceeding love and brotherly kindness. They held fast to each other and visited the sick fearlessly, and ministered to them continually, serving them in Christ. And they died with them most joyfully, taking the affliction of others, and drawing the sickness from their neighbors to themselves and willingly receiving their pains. And many who cared for the sick and gave strength to others died themselves having transferred to themselves their death...But with the heathen everything was quite otherwise. They deserted those who began to be sick, and fled from their dearest friends. And they cast them out into the streets when they were half dead, and left the dead like refuse, unburied.[2]

The early Christians ministered to and showed hospitality toward the poor, orphans, the elderly, the sick, mineworkers, and prisoners.[3] Throughout the following centuries, the church played a major role in community transformation and led the way in meeting social needs and curing social ills. Celtic Ireland, for example, was considered too barbaric for the Romans to conquer and civilize. But in the fifth century, during twenty-eight years of sustained ministry, Patrick (later known as Saint Patrick) and his band of followers "planted about 700 churches...and ordained perhaps 1,000 priests. Within his lifetime, 30 to 40 (or more) of Ireland's 150 tribes became substantially Christian."[4] But Patrick did more than plant churches. He was also committed to creating a better life for the Irish. "He was the first public man to speak and crusade against slavery. Within his lifetime, or soon after, 'the Irish slave trade came to a halt, and other forms of violence, such as murder and intertribal warfare decreased,' and his communities modeled the Christian way of faithfulness, generosity, and peace to all the Irish."[5]

Concern for the Poor
and Abolishing Slavery

William Wilberforce, a member of England's Parliament and a committed Christian, is best known for his tireless commitment to the abolition of slavery. He introduced his first bill to abolish slavery in the House of Commons in 1791. It was soundly defeated. Wilberforce continued to fight for the same cause for sixteen years until the slave trade in England was finally abolished in 1807.[6]

The revival and the Great Awakening of the 1700s included both the proclamation and demonstration of the gospel. The church took off the gloves and took on some of the toughest problems of the day. John Wesley (1703-1791), who led revivals in the eighteenth century, did more than just talk about social reform. Among other things, he campaigned for prison and labor reform, encouraged the building of orphanages and schools, battled against the slave trade, gave medicines and health treatment to the poor, worked to help resolve unemployment, set up accounts for making loans to the poor, and personally gave away considerable sums of money to people in need. Wesley exhorted his middle class followers, "If those who gain all they can, and save all they can, will likewise give all they can; then, the more they gain, the more they will grow in grace, and the more treasure they will lay up in heaven." [7]

In 1865 William and Catherine Booth began what became known as the Salvation Army. A contemporary wrote, "Probably during no hundred years in the history of the world have there been saved so many thieves, gamblers, drunkards, and prostitutes as during the past quarter of a century through the...Salvation Army." [8]

Christians have been at the forefront of establishing child-labor laws, schools, universities, orphanages, and hospitals...as well as aiding in famine relief, settlement houses, and rescue missions. Christian leaders such as William Booth and Jane Addams of Hull House in Chicago led the way in restoring the bodies and minds, as well as the souls, of those who were converted.

Although many secularists like to dismiss the Christian missionary movement as harmful to native cultures, the facts, in most cases, do not validate their suppositions. Historian David Bosch writes, "The missionary movement made a prime contribution to the abolition of slavery; spread better methods of agriculture; established…schools; gave medical care to millions; elevated the status of women; created bonds between people of different countries, which war could not sever; trained…the leadership of the nations now newly independent." [9]

What Good Deeds Accomplish

My car came to a stop as I (Eric) queued up to turn off the freeway. The beat-up station wagon in front of me seemed to be held together with bumper stickers espousing everything from "Visualize Whirled Peas" to "Born Once Is Enough for Me" to "Don't Blame Me. I Voted for Mondale." (It was an old car.) But the most prominent sticker, prominently displayed under the rear window, read, "Do Something Really Radical—Practice Your Religion." Now there's an

It is our actions toward others that separate Christianity from philosophy.

idea…people actually expect us to live out our faith. And the fella was right.

The Christian faith, for the most part, has been reduced to a philosophy—principles and tenets that we believe and can defend but don't necessarily practice. It is our actions toward others that separate Christianity from philosophy. It is tying *loving God* to *loving our neighbors as ourselves* that puts legs to our faith. So let's be radicals and practice our religion. First let's look at what good deeds accomplish.

Good Deeds Genuinely Benefit Others

"Let us do good to all people" (from Galatians 6:10). Good deeds are not just the wrapping for the gospel. Make no mistake about it—acts of love, mercy, compassion, and justice really help others and move them toward physical and emotional wholeness in a broken world. Giving water to the thirsty, food to the hungry, clothing to the shivering, companionship to the lonely, health to the sick, and hospitality to the stranger are all things God cares deeply about. Ministering to others is something the Lord requires of us, whether those to whom we minister come to faith or not. The stipulation for loving and serving is not that they come to faith or attend our church. We love and serve because we are followers of Christ. The Apostle John writes, "If anyone has material possessions and sees his brother in need but has no pity on him, how can the love of God be in him? Dear children, let us not love with words or tongue but with actions and in truth" (1 John 3:17-18). Pastor Charles Roesel of First Baptist Church in Leesburg, Florida, says, "Evangelism that does not minister to the needs of the whole person falls short of the New Testament standard."[10] Hosea 11:4 says, "I led them with cords of human kindness, with ties of love." People often are led to God by humans who show them love and kindness. Your ministry to others may be the beginning of a reconciling relationship with God.

Good Deeds Glorify God

Good deeds magnify the character of God. "Let your light shine before men, that they may see your good deeds and praise your Father in heaven" (Matthew 5:16). Jesus' good works brought praise and glory to the Father (Luke 5:25-26). During the great plague that occurred during the reign of Roman Emperor Maximinus Daza (A.D. 309-313), the church historian Eusebius wrote of how Christians responded to the tragedy. Eusebius pointed out that it was during this dark time that the Christians' light shone the brightest and brought the goodness of God into the light:

> Then did they show themselves to the heathen in the clearest light. For the Christians were the only people who amid such terrible ills showed their fellow-feeling and humanity by their actions. Day by day some would busy themselves with attending to the dead and burying them (for there were numbers to whom no one else paid any heed); others gathered in one spot all who were afflicted by hunger throughout the whole city and gave bread to them all. When this became known, *people glorified the Christians' God,* and, convinced by the very facts, confessed the Christians alone were truly pious and religious.[11]

Good Deeds Validate the Good News

The paralyzed man was lowered through the ceiling and put before Jesus. Jesus, seeing the faith of his friends, said, "Friend, your sins are forgiven." The religious leaders were dumbfounded. "Who can forgive sins but God alone?" Jesus answered that it was the good deeds that validate the good news. " 'But that you may know that the Son of Man has authority on earth to forgive sins...' he said to the paralyzed man, 'I tell you, get up, take up your mat and go home.' Immediately he stood up in front of them...and went home praising God" (Luke 5:20-25).

> **Take away service, and you take away the church's power, influence, and evangelistic effectiveness.**

When the Communists took over Russia in 1917, they vigorously persecuted the church but did not make Christianity illegal. The Constitution of 1918 (chapter 5, article 13), in fact, guaranteed a freedom of religion. But the Communists did make it illegal for the church to do any good works. No longer could the church fulfill its historic role of feeding the hungry, educating the young, housing the orphan, or caring for the sick. The state would handle those duties. What was the result? After seventy years, the church in Russia was largely irrelevant to the communities in which it dwelt. Take away service, and you take away the church's power, influence, and evangelistic effectiveness. The power of the gospel is combining its life-changing message with selfless service. Have we done by default what Lenin did by diabolic design? Have we disengaged from our communities and therefore become irrelevant to them?

Today we live in a world that is often referred to as postmodern. The "modern" age began with the Enlightenment and the Age of Reason. Educated people believed that philosophical and moral truth, like laws of science, could be discovered through logic and laws of noncontradiction. The postmodern world is quite different. It is widely held that there are many interpretations of truth, with no one truth prevailing. In America fewer people are coming to faith through the old methods. People want more than arguments for faith; they want proof of faith. We need an apologetic for faith that can be *observed* more than postulated and debated.

Good Deeds Move People Toward Jesus

If *servant evangelism* were a phrase in the dictionary, there would be a picture of Steve Sjogren next to it. The founding pastor of Vineyard Community Church in Cincinnati, Ohio, Steve is all about showing the love of Christ with no strings attached. "It's not so much a matter of sharing information as it is sharing love," he explains.

Steve's church sees hundreds of people come to Christ every year. Every Saturday morning the people of the church set aside a couple of hours to do simple acts of service to the community...things that anyone can do. They give free car washes in the summer, wrap Christmas presents at the mall, and do scores of other service projects in between. Joining with other churches last summer, they handed out 300,000 soft drinks and bottles of water in a single day just to demonstrate God's love and concern for the people of Cincinnati. Frequently, between Sunday morning services, one of the pastors will grab a bag of groceries and a new Christian and deliver the groceries to a family in the community. Service is a way of life at Vineyard. When people are served and loved and they *see* good deeds, they are more apt to want to *hear* the good news behind it. Good works create enormous curiosity that begs to be satisfied with deeper understanding and conversations about spiritual matters. For many people, being on the receiving end of good deeds is often their introduction to the church.

> **We need an apologetic for faith that can be observed more than postulated and debated.**

Good Deeds Create Goodwill With the City

Calvary Bible Church sits right outside the city limits of Boulder, Colorado. For years the people of the church have tried to connect the church to the city's water supply because their own well water is virtually depleted. A couple of years ago, senior pastor Tom Shirk, along with a few church leaders, attended a city council meeting at which their request for annexation was in the final stage of consideration. The council was reviewing all the potential effects the annexation would have on the city and surrounding neighborhoods. During the discussion, one city councilman

Good News and Good Deeds • **119**

church property on an oversized map and said, "Now we ⸍is church being here forever, so we should designate this ₒₙ-density residential land now so that when the church is no ₙere, the property will be properly zoned." When it was Tom's turn ₜo speak, he said that he envisioned his church or some church being on the property for quite a long time. The councilman responded that the city allocates land use for the benefit of all the community and asked Tom, "What benefit will the annexation of this property have for our city?" He wasn't mean-spirited, and since he and the others are the elected stewards of the land, it was within his purview to ask the question.

Knowing that housing issues are at the top of the city's concerns, Tom responded that three years ago the church had spent $40,000 and used sixty volunteers to construct a Habitat for Humanity house. The church had also provided the lion's share of labor in refurbishing a home for runaway youth in the city. For the past two years, the church had served as an overflow facility for the city's homeless shelter. The councilman responded, "We didn't know your church was doing all this good. I suppose that by providing shelter for the homeless, one could argue that the church is actually providing affordable housing." That evening the city council voted unanimously to extend the water line nearly a quarter of a mile to the church. Good deeds get noticed.

What Good Deeds Do Not Accomplish

Good deeds help people and communities in need. Good deeds can engender the goodwill of the city. Good deeds can get people to think about faith and be willing to hear more. Good deeds can elicit amazement and cause people to say "Wow!" Good deeds can draw people into your church and into relationships with Christians. But good deeds, in spite of all the wonderful things they can accomplish, are not sufficient to lead a person to saving faith in Jesus. Good works can be the bridge or the road, but they are not the saving message that crosses that bridge or travels that road. Good works are the complement but never the substitute for good news.

Remember, it is the *gospel* (literally, "good news") that is "the power of God for the salvation of everyone who believes" (Romans 1:16). "Faith comes from hearing the message, and the message is heard through the word of Christ" (Romans 10:17). If we care about people coming to Christ, we must figure out ways to be intentional about evangelism—sharing the good news. Saint Francis of Assisi is credited with the statement "Preach Christ at all times and when necessary use words." If we think it is *necessary* for people to understand the gospel, then we've got to use words. Many people like to point out that Jesus used the word *kingdom* many more times than he used the word *salvation*, and thus they argue that it's all about the kingdom. But it's hard to bring in the kingdom without telling people that there is a King. In *The Urban Face of Mission,* Susan Baker writes, "Many churches have…outreach ministries. All too often, such ministries slip into meeting the designated need without the participants ever hearing that this is an expression of the love of a God who wants them to be his children and wants to transform their lives."[12]

If we care about people coming to Christ, we must figure out ways to be intentional about evangelism—sharing the good news.

The Tyranny of the "Or"— the Genius of the "And"

A few years ago, an insightful best seller was written by Jim Collins and Jerry Porras titled *Built to Last: Successful Habits of Visionary Companies.* The authors introduced the concept that most companies live in the "tyranny of the or": either-or dichotomies that force the choice between profit and benefit to society, between speed and quality, and so on. Collins and Porras point out that successful companies actually pursue two seemingly contrary goals simultaneously: profit *and* idealism, speed of production *and* quality of product.[13]

One day Jesus was confronted by a group of Pharisees (Matthew 22:34-39). "Teacher, which is the greatest commandment in the Law?" one of them asked. Refusing to be caught up in their trickery, Jesus gave them two equally important answers: " 'Love the Lord your God with all your heart and with all your soul and with all your mind.' This is the first and greatest

commandment. And the second is like it: 'Love your neighbor as yourself.' "
Jesus would not submit to the "tyranny of the 'or.' " A life of faith must always
give primacy to loving God *and* loving people—the "genius of the 'and.' "

In the same way, churches don't
have to choose either good news *or*
good deeds, initiating service *or* initiating evangelism. They also don't have
to choose to either build up the church

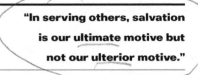

**"In serving others, salvation
is our ultimate motive but
not our ulterior motive."**

or do externally focused ministry. Churches can pursue both at the same
time. It is in turning the "or" into an "and" that God shows up, creativity is
found, and breakthrough ministry ideas are discovered.

Sam Williams says, "In serving others, salvation is our *ultimate* motive
but not our *ulterior* motive. People sniff out motives pretty quickly."
However, like Paul, whose "heart's desire and prayer...is that they may be
saved" (Romans 10:1), we'd be less than honest to claim that we don't care
if people come to Christ. But our condition for helping and serving, or con-
tinuing to do so, is not that people come to faith. We serve because serving
is at the core of our being, the reflection of who we are as Christ-followers.
Getting to share the gospel is not a condition of our service, but service
often creates wonderful opportunities to share the gospel.

How Do We Share the Good News?

Serving others puts us automatically into relationships with those we are
serving and those with whom we are serving. Pastor Chip Sweney of
Perimeter Church in Atlanta says, "As we serve those in need, it opens the
door to share about the hope that we have. People's hearts are open when
they see that you really care about them and their needs. Just the fact that
you are serving will provoke questions for which you must have answers."[14]

Peter captures the link between service and evangelism in this passage
from 1 Peter 3:13-15: "Who is going to harm you if you are eager to do
good... But in your hearts set apart Christ as Lord. Always be prepared to
give an answer to everyone who asks you to give the reason for the hope
that you have." Peter says from experience that doing good will provoke
many spiritual conversations. Trained Christians work and pray toward

all members trained to tell the good news

sharing Christ with their non-Christian friends. All church members should therefore be trained in telling their faith stories and the basics of the gospel message. Service tees up the opportunity, but you've got to swing the club. "How, then, can they call on the one they have not believed in? And how can they believe in the one of whom they have not heard? And how can they hear without someone preaching to them?" (Romans 10:14). Eventually someone has to move out in faith and share the gospel.

Three Stories

How can we tell others the good news? We suggest you think in terms of stories.

First, listen to the other person's story. As you listen, look for evidence of God working in the person's life. Learn to ask good questions, questions that will help the individual tell the story and draw out his or her spiritual journey. Here are some examples: "Where are you in your spiritual journey?" "What words would you use to describe your spiritual life?" "Do you find yourself wanting to move closer to God or away from God? Why?" "If you could ask God one question, what would it be?" Questions like these are windows into the soul.

> **Service tees up the opportunity, but you've got to swing the club.**

Second, ask permission to tell your story. "May I tell you a little of my story (or spiritual journey)?" Asking permission demonstrates respect and deference. Your story is your testimony: your life before you met Christ, how you met Christ, and the difference he has made in your life. Talk about the areas of life change that intersect with the story of the individual to whom you're talking.

Third, ask permission to tell God's story: the plan of salvation. "If you're interested, at some time I'd like to show you a diagram, booklet, concept—whatever method you want to use to present the gospel that has really helped me understand what it means to have a relationship with God." By saying, "some time," you take the pressure off. He or she can say yes or no without jeopardizing the relationship. But an affirmative response sets you up to share the gospel at a future time (and also gives you time to prepare for the conversation). If the person agrees, you can say something like "How about if I come by on Tuesday about this time, and we can go grab a cup of coffee?"

Remember, evangelism is 90 percent God's part and 10 percent our part. God is the one who draws people to himself (John 6:65) and does all the preparation so that people aren't *forced* to believe but *want* to believe.

I (Eric) wear two contact lenses. One allows me to see objects that are far away. The other allows me to see things that are nearby, such as a computer screen or my dinner. When I look through both eyes, I can't distinguish which lens allows me to see up close and which one allows me to see far away. It's only when I close one eye that I realize what the other eye sees. That's probably how it should be when Christians look at others' needs. We need to see their physical needs as well as their spiritual needs without closing either eye.

It's Tough Out There Today

In many secularized communities, traditional ways of reaching people have run their course and are no longer effective. Four years ago I (Eric) went door to door to twenty-five homes as part of a citywide evangelistic initiative. The strategy was simple: I was to smile, introduce myself, and ask if I could give them a free video of the *Jesus* film—one of the most watched films in history. I've had the pleasure of sharing Christ with lots of people and have seen many come to faith; so, armed with prayer and hopefulness, I started knocking. How did I do? I was zero for twenty-five.

I won't try to spiritualize this through a homily on the importance of just being faithful. I felt like a big *loser!* Common sense tells me to quit long before I go zero for twenty-five. But I was trying to *give* something away— something beneficial, something spiritual. And I was experienced. At the last five houses, I just prayed that no one would be home. I hated the rejection.

Ever feel that way? Maybe we need to explore some new evangelistic strategies. Evangelism doesn't have to be reduced to doing something you don't like with people you don't know. Imagine how much more motivating it would be for those in your church if people were saying, "Thanks for coming by. You're really making a difference in our town. I don't go to church, but if I did, I'd like to go to one like yours." Do you think they'd be encouraged? Externally focused churches are discovering approaches that give them great favor with their communities. Externally focused churches are trying to position themselves so that everyone in their communities knows someone who follows Jesus.

> **Evangelism doesn't have to be reduced to doing something you don't like with people you don't know.**

Four Types of Churches

To help you determine your church's current focus, we've developed the following graph. Take a look at the four quadrants. The vertical axis represents good deeds. The horizontal axis represents good news. The midway point of each axis separates internal focus from external focus.

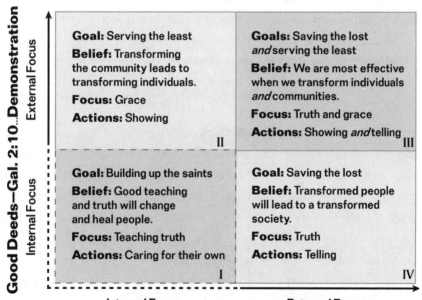

Good Deeds—Gal. 2:10...Demonstration

External Focus

II

Goal: Serving the least
Belief: Transforming the community leads to transforming individuals.
Focus: Grace
Actions: Showing

III

Goals: Saving the lost *and* serving the least
Belief: We are most effective when we transform individuals *and* communities.
Focus: Truth and grace
Actions: Showing *and* telling

Internal Focus

I

Goal: Building up the saints
Belief: Good teaching and truth will change and heal people.
Focus: Teaching truth
Actions: Caring for their own

IV

Goal: Saving the lost
Belief: Transformed people will lead to a transformed society.
Focus: Truth
Actions: Telling

Internal Focus   External Focus

Good News—Romans 1:15...Proclamation

Internally focused churches (Quadrant I)—These churches are good at preaching and teaching, worship, and serving the needs of those *inside* the church. Many of the great churches today fit this model. These churches excel in pastoral care and building up the saints. When people come to these churches, they will hear biblical truth and the message of salvation, and they will see people coming to know the Lord. The distinguishing characteristic is that these churches are "come to" churches. They find themselves asking, "How can we meet the needs 'out there' when we have so many needs 'in here'?" Look at some characteristics of internally focused churches:

Goal: Building up the saints

Belief: Good teaching and truth will change and heal people.

Focus: Teaching truth

Actions: Caring for their own

Serving churches (Quadrant II)—These churches are really good at demonstrating love for their communities. They've been at the forefront of bringing social and systemic change to the cities but are weak in proclaiming the gospel. Characteristics of serving churches include:

Goal: Serving the least

Belief: Transforming the community leads to transforming individuals.

Focus: Grace

Actions: Showing

Externally focused churches (Quadrant III)—These churches are effective in proclaiming good news *and* showing love to their communities. They are not caught up in the "tyranny of the 'or.' " They don't believe that you have to compromise truth to show grace. Jesus, after all, was full of both grace and truth. The gospel for these churches is both show and tell. Here are some of their characteristics:

Goals: Saving the lost *and* serving the least

Belief: We are most effective when we transform individuals *and* communities.

Focus: Truth *and* grace

Actions: Showing *and* telling

Evangelistic churches (Quadrant IV)—This breed of church is becoming increasingly scarce. It focuses on evangelism outside the church. For these churches it's all about going after the lost. They may reach into their communities by going door to door, handing out literature, or sponsoring evangelistic crusades. But they do little or nothing to serve or to be a blessing to their communities apart from evangelism. They are convinced that evangelism is the most important thing they can be doing, and if this strategy is working, may they keep moving ahead. We need more churches and people committed to initiative evangelism. Some characteristics of these churches include:

Goal: Saving the lost

Belief: Transformed people will lead to a transformed society.

Focus: Truth

Actions: Telling

Externally focused churches have discovered that they don't have to compromise telling the truth to demonstrate grace. They have discovered the ministry style of Jesus. He didn't compromise the good news to engage in good deeds. He didn't compromise saving the lost by serving the least. He didn't compromise truth in his grace or grace in his truth.

Today we need a new generation of Christ-followers filling externally focused churches—people who can think and act with the same combination of complexity and simplicity, bringing grace *and* truth, individual transformation *and* community transformation, good news *and* good deeds to those around them…with the hopeful expectation that they are changing the world.

Something to **Think** About

"An individual gospel without a social gospel is a soul without a body and a social gospel without an individual gospel is a body without a soul. One is a ghost and the other a corpse."[15]

—E. Stanley Jones

Something to **Talk** About

Where is your church? Review the graph on page 125. Draw a circle that encompasses the ministries of your church. Most likely you will want to draw some type of ellipse containing parts of more than one quadrant (for example, your church may be mostly in Quadrant I but partially in Quadrant IV).

- Quadrant I churches are good at preaching and teaching and are helpful to those inside their church. They "take care of their own" to one degree or another. When people come to this type of church, they will hear the message of salvation, and they will see people coming to know the Lord. These are "come to" churches.

- Quadrant II churches are externally focused on evangelism. They may reach into their communities by going door to door, handing out literature, or sponsoring an evangelistic crusade. But they do little or nothing to be a blessing to their communities.

- Quadrant III churches are effective in proclaiming good news *and* showing love to their communities.

- Quadrant IV churches are really good at demonstrating love for their communities, but they are weak in proclaiming the gospel.

Ask participants to show where they drew their circles on the graph and explain why they characterized your church as they did.

Something to **Act** Upon

1. List the ministries and service opportunities that your church or you personally are involved in.

2. Where have you been caught up in the "tyranny of the 'or' "—excluding service in order to do evangelism or excluding evangelism in order to serve?

3. Knowing that breakthrough ideas come from changing the "or" to an "and," what could you do to instill a mind-set that embraces both service and evangelism in your church?

4. Train each of your small groups in using the "Three Stories" model of evangelism, which includes training in telling God's story (the gospel).

Sermon/**Lesson** Idea

Text: Luke 4:16-19; Isaiah 61:1-6

Main Idea: When Jesus gave his first public sermon in his hometown of Nazareth, he used Isaiah 61 as his text. From this passage he explains his ministry focus and strategy. Notice the integration of his oral message and his helpful service. Jesus' ministry would always focus on good news *and* good deeds.

Illustration: The genius of the "and"

Action Point: Have members of each ministry team in the church work through how they can be intentional about evangelism and service in every program or tactic in which they are involved.

Endnotes

1. http://www.famous-quotations.com/forum/forum_posts.asp?TID=274&get=last

2. http://www.newadvent.org/fathers/250107.htm, from *Church History* by Eusebius, Book VII, Chapter 22.

3. Adolf Harnack, *The Expansion of Christianity in the First Three Centuries, vol. 1* (Eugene, OR: Wipf and Stock Publishers, 1998), 189-190.

4. George G. Hunter III, *The Celtic Way of Evangelism* (Nashville, TN: Abingdon Press, 2000), 22-23.

5. Ibid. Interior quote is from Thomas Cahill, *How the Irish Saved Civilization,* 110.

6. http://www.baobab.or.jp/~stranger/character/wilber.htm

7. http://www.onemethodist.com/Vol3No09.htm

8. Josiah Strong, as quoted in Norris Magnuson, *Salvation in the Slums: Evangelical Social Work, 1865-1920* (Metuchen, NJ: The Scarecrow Press, Inc., 1977), 7.

9. David J. Bosch, *Transforming Mission* (Maryknoll, NY: Orbis Books, 1991), 294.

10. Charles Roesel, comments (Leesburg, FL: conversation with Eric Swanson, April 8, 2003).

11. Harnack, *The Expansion of Christianity in the First Three Centuries, vol. 1*, 214-215.

12. Susan S. Baker, "The Social Sciences: Tools for Urban Ministry," from *The Urban Face of Mission* by Harvie M. Conn (Phillipsburg, NJ: P&R Publishing Company, 2002), 81.

13. James C. Collins and Jerry I. Porras, *Built to Last: Successful Habits of Visionary Companies* (New York: Harper Business, 1994), 43-45.

14. Chip Sweney, comments (Irvine, CA: conversation with Eric Swanson, November 4, 2003).

15. E. Stanley Jones, *The Unshakable Kingdom and the Unchanging Person* (Nashville, TN: Abingdon Press, 1972), 40.

---

chapter | **seven**

From **Mercy** to **Justice**

"There's a hole in the world tonight. There's a cloud of fear and sorrow. There's a hole in the world tonight. Don't let there be a hole in the world tomorrow."

—The Eagles

Learn What This Means

In the ninth chapter of his Gospel, Matthew records, in an understated way, the day he met Jesus. "As Jesus went on from there, he saw a man named Matthew sitting at the tax collector's booth. 'Follow me,' he told him, and Matthew got up and followed him" (Matthew 9:9). Out of gratitude for his new friend, Matthew threw a party at his house; in fact, Luke called it a "great banquet for Jesus" (Luke 5:29). And who else did Matthew invite to this great party? His buddies, of course—"many tax collectors and 'sinners' " (Matthew 9:10). He wanted them to meet his new friend. Jesus' disciples were also invited and joined in the festivities. (New Christ-followers are usually great at throwing parties, and they are the ones with all the non-Christian friends!)

But another group was also present...maybe not inside the house but certainly peering through the windows or standing at the doorway. These were the Pharisees. The Pharisees were big on separating themselves from anything or anyone that would defile them, so they usually didn't get many invitations to the really good parties. A Pharisee was an expert in distinguishing between the clean and the unclean, between the righteous and the sinners. The Pharisees thought they had the inside scoop on God's way to do everything, and they left little margin for disagreement. Observing Jesus freely hanging around tax collectors and sinners was a major problem for these separatists. They didn't have a category for this man from Nazareth. So they cornered Jesus' disciples and asked, " 'Why does your teacher eat with tax collectors and "sinners"?' On hearing this, Jesus said, 'It is not the healthy who need a doctor, but the sick. But go and learn what this means: "I desire mercy, not sacrifice." For I have not come to call the righteous, but sinners' " (Matthew 9:11b-13).

With these words, Jesus revealed his life's purpose and his values, and he invited those within the sound of his voice to deepen their understanding. He referred to a Scripture that we need to understand if we are to live as Jesus lived: "I desire mercy, not sacrifice." Interestingly, this is the only recorded teaching of Jesus in which he tells someone to "go and learn" the meaning of a scriptural passage.

Grazing on the Sabbath

Hold your finger in the Matthew 9 passage, turn a few pages to Matthew 12, and read verses 1-7. Jesus' disciples were hungry and were picking grain for a ready-made snack. Technically, they were doing work on the Sabbath. Again the Pharisees confronted Jesus. "Look! Your disciples are doing what is unlawful on the Sabbath." Not to be trapped, Jesus responded by citing some biblical and historical precedents and then said, "If you had known what these words mean, 'I desire mercy, not sacrifice,' you would not have condemned the innocent." Clearly, the Pharisees had not learned the lesson that Jesus had told them to "go and learn" at Matthew's house. The verse from the Old Testament that Jesus cited on both occasions seems to be one important key to understanding Jesus' heart.

Understanding Mercy

The passage that Jesus refers to is in Hosea 6:6: "For I desire mercy, not sacrifice." What is mercy? Mercy, most simply put, is God's attitude and action toward those in need or in distress. Mercy goes beyond pity (to feel sorry for) or compassion (to feel sorry with). Mercy is always expressed in actions. The story of the good Samaritan illustrates the difference between pity and mercy. The Samaritan distinguished himself from the priest and the Levite not just because he "took pity on him" (Luke 10:33) but also because he "had mercy on him" (Luke 10:37). Mercy is love with legs on it.

Mercy is love with legs on it.

Giving Them a Name

The world can be a cold place in which people separate themselves from others on the basis of economic conditions, ethnicity, or fortune. It's easy to think of people in need as part of a faceless, nameless mass of humanity. People are much more real to us when we know their names. A name carries with it a sense of value, identity, belonging, and connection. To know a person by name signifies some type of relationship beyond a label or classification.

Recently a friend who runs a ministry to the homeless in an affluent city in Southern California received a copy of an irate letter from one of the ministry center's neighbors. The neighbor had addressed the letter to the mayor and had sent copies to our friend, to a city councilman, and to the police chief. In it, she described the people at the ministry center as homeless, drunks, drug users, prostitutes, and loiterers. Here is how our friend responded:

> Thank you for the copy of your recent letter to our mayor concerning our neighborhood. I share your concern for the well-being of our neighborhood and our neighbors. I would like to share with you what we do at [the ministry center] on Sunday evenings and how it impacts the people that you described in your letter.
>
> Last Sunday we met at [the ministry center] (normally we meet there on the first Sunday of the month and the rest of the month we meet at the church), and everyone there joined in prayer before

our meal. We enjoyed a wonderful meal together, and afterward about twenty of the folks that you wrote about in your letter met in the back yard for a Bible study discipleship class and a time of prayer. A few of the sports-minded men stayed inside and watched the NBA playoff game between the Spurs and the Nets.

Just as I finished the Bible study, a homeless family from Iran walked up. We not only connected Zumi and her family with a motel room, but also connected them with an Iranian church that can help them get on their feet.

As we closed with prayer, a tall, strong African-American man named John walked up and shared with me that he was tired of the street and his crack cocaine addiction and wanted help. He had just wandered into town from Florida via San Bernardino.

I loaded up the van and my car and took a previously homeless family consisting of Mom, Dad, and nine children—Vanessa, Valerie, Olivia, Daniel, Christian, Eric, Dawn, and the twins, Michael and Isaiah—back to the home that our church had found for them in Rancho Cucamonga. When I returned to [the ministry center], I met with John who wanted rest and rescue from his addiction.

As I was locking the gate, a woman walked by cursing to herself. She saw me and apologized, and I asked her if she was OK. She said she was upset that she was on the street, that she had been robbed, and that her supposed "friends" told her they would give her some money if she provided them with sexual favors. She had told them no and had walked away from them in disgust. This was the first time I had met this woman. Her name is Sherry. I told her that she could always come to me if she needed help, and that I was proud of her for walking away from her "friends." She said she just wanted to go home to Reno, Nevada. I told her to meet with me Tuesday morning at my office, and that I would help her get home.

After she left I drove the addicted man, John, down to skid row to look for a place to get him help, but everything was full. I called a friend in another town who took him in and took him to drug treatment at 6:30 a.m. Monday.

This morning I bought a bus ticket for Sherry, who will leave for Reno, Nevada, today. I gave her some food money. We called her aunt in Nevada and asked her to meet Sherry at the bus station.

I am sharing this just to tell you a little bit about the people we serve at the church and at [the ministry center] and what we do when we encounter them and their challenging situations.

Thanks again,

Andy

Andy sees each of these people as someone God loves and Jesus died for. Names, not case numbers, will be written in the Book of Life. There will be Johns and Zumis and Vanessas and Valeries and Sherrys and Akbars and Jamals and Rasheeds and Martas and Diegos—each person will have a name. Andy knows the names of the people that he ministers to because he knows them. Maybe putting a name to a face won't change them, but it has changed Andy.

Mercy is giving a person a fish so he can eat today. It's not attacking problems at the systemic level. It's just making someone's life better, if only for today. Mercy explains why Jesus so willingly fed the five thousand (the only miracle recorded in all four Gospels) and later the four thousand. He didn't lecture them about how to plant wheat for a future harvest. Rather, he said, "I have compassion for these people...I do not want to send them away hungry" (Matthew 15:32). He did not solve the world's hunger problem, but he did make these people's lives better for that afternoon.

Sometimes we are paralyzed by inaction. Faced with the enormous problems in our world today, we are overwhelmed and wonder, "What good will this little act of kindness do?" But Jesus said, "Be merciful, just as your Father is merciful" (Luke 6:36). Maybe Mother Teresa expressed it best: "We can do no great things; only small things with great love."[1]

In your community, are there any who are hungry or thirsty? Are there any who are strangers? Are there any who lack clothing or are sick? Are there any who are incarcerated? Every time you do something as simple as giving someone a cup of water or a cup of hot coffee in the name of Jesus, you help to make the kingdom of God visible.

Mercy and Justice

Mercy differs from justice just as democracy differs from liberty. Jack Jezreel, founder of JustFaith, illustrates the difference between mercy and justice this way:

> Suppose one morning I wake up, look out my window, and in the stream that runs behind my house I see a man who is unconscious, wet, and bleeding? Of course I'd rush to his aid and give him medical attention and get him to the hospital. What if the next day I find another man in the stream in the same condition? Well, I'd also take care of him. But if on the third day I found another person, after getting that person to the hospital, I'd better walk upriver and find out how and why these bodies are getting into the stream![2]

To take care of the wounded is charity. To walk up the river to see why the person is wounded is to begin the search for justice. *Justice* is "the quality of being just" or "conformity to moral rightness in action or attitude." Even in the early days of the faith, the church made the distinction between mercy and justice. The first deacons were selected to rectify an injustice— the Grecian "widows were being overlooked in the daily distribution of food" (Acts 6:1). The apostles found the source of the problem and appointed seven men to identify and implement a solution to ensure that the widows were treated justly.

The late Harvie Conn defines the distinction between charity and justice and in so doing asks, "What will be the instrument of the church in effecting...change? Not simply charity but also justice. Charity is episodic, justice is ongoing. One brings consolation, the other correction. One aims at symptoms, the other at causes. One changes individuals, the other societies."[3]

Act Justly, Love Mercy, Walk Humbly

There are many good things Christians can do to help and serve others. We need more acts of mercy and charity to salve the wounds of the world around us. Acts of service that demonstrate the love of God and move people toward Jesus are vital. But perhaps they are not enough. The prophet Micah reminds us of the three things God requires of us: "to act justly and to love mercy and to walk humbly with [our] God" (Micah 6:8).

Most evangelical churches help people know Christ and walk humbly with God. The church makes a critical transition when it looks outside its four walls and begins to extend mercy to those around it. This is the first step in becoming an externally focused church. But to act justly is much more difficult, for it seeks to address underlying causes more than symptoms.

Humility, Mercy, and Justice

It's important to understand the levels of complexity and degree of difficulty in moving from a humble walk to mercy and justice. The following is a chart that may help you visualize the Micah 6:8 blueprint.

Walk Humbly With God	Love Mercy	Act Justly
Addresses the spiritual lives of those who come to church • Personal salvation • Spiritual disciplines • Seeking the Lord • Worship • Becoming a devoted follower	Addresses individual symptoms of those outside the church • Acts of kindness • Giving people "fish" 　Shelter 　Groceries 　Clothing 　Medical care	Addresses causes that create symptoms • Teaching people how to fish and how to own the pond 　Evangelism/discipleship 　Tutoring/mentoring 　Job training 　Job/business creation 　Livable wages 　Home ownership
Internally Focused	**Externally Focused**	**Externally Focused**

Looking at the above chart, one can see that most of our finest churches are in the "Walk Humbly With God" column. They offer wonderful worship opportunities and are great at proclaiming the Word, and they help people with their personal lives, their marriages, their identities, and their lifestyles. In coming to know Jesus, their people begin to experience peace where once they experienced frustration. They live in forgiveness where once they experienced guilt. They live with purpose instead of aimlessness.

But the efforts of many of these churches remain largely inside their four walls. They have embraced one of God's "desires" described in Micah 6:8 (to walk humbly) but have neglected the other two (loving mercy and acting justly). Christ did not come into our lives just to make us better but also to give us the power to make the world a better place through our ministry and service to others.

All of us who know Christ personally would say that he has radically changed our lives. But often we limit these changes to what Christ does *in* us without allowing him to work *through* us. To belong to Christ, to be adopted into his family, is to begin to care about what he cares about—to move outside of ourselves and toward others in mercy and justice.

Fish

An old Chinese proverb says…"Give a man a fish, and you will feed him for a day. Teach a man to fish, and you will feed him for a lifetime." (That is assuming he likes sushi. If he doesn't, then you have to teach him how to cook.) There are many churches that are satisfied with giving people what they need for their daily sustenance. Giving a man a fish is an act of mercy. Teaching a man to fish is to move toward justice. Helping people become self-sustaining is nothing short of transformational.

Think of the people that Jesus encountered. Among them were the blind, the lame, the deaf, the lepers, and the demon possessed. Apart from their physical infirmities, those with compelling physical needs faced at least two other problems. First, they were most often unable to work and so lived in dependence on others. Second, they were excluded from the social and spiritual life of the community (Leviticus 13–15). They were disenfranchised. They were outcasts longing to be in the mainstream. Every time Jesus healed someone of a debilitating illness, he was empowering him or her not just for a day but also for a lifetime. It was Jesus' way of teaching these people to fish—to move from dependence (and being in constant need of mercy) to sufficiency.

In 1999, twenty-five volunteers from Hope Presbyterian Church in Memphis paired up with twenty-five inner-city children in the first through the fifth grade. The children's reading skills were tested before the program began. After reading with the Hope volunteers for just twelve weeks, these children raised their reading scores by 1.2 grades! As of this writing, one hundred volunteers from Hope regularly read to children in South Memphis.[4] They are teaching these children how to fish.

Helping People Own the Pond

In 1987 Luis Cortés, working with other clergy in North Philadelphia, began Nueva Esperanza (New Hope) "to improve the quality of life in our community through the development of Hispanic-owned and -operated educational, economic, and spiritual institutions." They began with a proposition that went beyond handing out fish and teaching men to fish. Instead, they thought, "Think of the difference it would make if we helped people own the pond!" In Philadelphia the average net wealth of a Latino family is a mere $4,000 compared to the $44,000 of an Anglo family. Recognizing that 60 percent of personal wealth is generally held in home equity, the people of Nueva Esperanza decided to help people own their own homes. To date this innovative ministry has built or refurbished more than 150 homes, which it has then sold to Latinos at cost; helped 650 families obtain first mortgages; and provided mortgage counseling to over 2,500 people. In addition, they have served hundreds of families in their Welfare to Work initiative.[5] They are helping their neighbors "own the pond" by enabling them to own the assets that lead to self-sufficiency.

It Doesn't Have to Be the Same Poor

God says, "There will always be poor people in the land. Therefore I command you to be openhanded toward your brothers and toward the poor and needy in your land" (Deuteronomy 15:11). There will always be poor in the land, but must they always be the *same* poor? It could be argued that financial poverty is a stage most people pass through as a normal stage of life. When you were a child, you had no assets. If you were a college student, working your way through college, you had nothing but debt. If your kids are in college now and they are broke and no one seems to be concerned, it's because most recognize this as a healthy stage in life during which they learn the skills necessary to move forward. In working with the poor, we need to be vigilant to not inadvertently perpetuate and facilitate poverty. Instead, we must help the poor obtain the skills and relationships necessary to move out of poverty.

The early church was charitable to all but moved people from dependence to sufficiency as quickly as possible. Church historian Adolf Harnack writes about the practical help the church offered.

> They formed a guild of workers, in the sense that the churches had to provide work for a brother whenever he required it. This fact seems…of great importance, from the social standpoint. The churches were also labor unions…The church did become in this way a refuge for people in distress, who were prepared to work. Its attractive power was consequently intensified, and from the economic standpoint we must attach very high value to a union which provided work for those who were able to work, and at the same time kept hunger from those who were unfit for any labor. [6]

God tells his people, "There should be no poor among you" (Deuteronomy 15:4a). Being involved with a community of faith should make a difference. Yes, there will always be poor in the land—a steady influx of immigrants and people who have suffered financial reversals because of tragedy or downturns in the economy. But the church, through mercy and justice, can help to ensure that these people don't stay poor.

If Your Church Left Town, Would Anybody Notice?

In 1988 Vaughn and Narlene McLaughlin moved into a depressed area of Jacksonville, Florida, to begin a church designed to meet the needs of the whole person. Vaughn didn't grow up going to church, so he was unconstrained by traditional ideas of what a church could be. Vaughn and Narlene soon discovered that beginning an innovative church isn't easy. As Vaughn expressed interest in purchasing an empty building, he was met with racial hatred, but he courageously pushed forward. Praise God he did. Today the Potter's House Christian Fellowship is a vibrant church of over three thousand people.

Vaughn had dreams, but he wanted to help others realize their dreams too. Recognizing that most new businesses fail because they are undercapitalized, the Potter's House does what it can to help potential businesses during the critical incubation period. Today their converted Southern Bell building, called the Multiplex, houses nearly twenty for-profit businesses begun by budding entrepreneurs from the church. The Multiplex is the home of the Potter's House Café, a credit union, a beauty salon, a graphic-design studio, a shoe-repair store, a travel agency, a Greyhound Bus terminal, and several other businesses, all started by church members who lacked capital but had a dream. Recently they purchased and are in the process of restoring and rebuilding the Normandy Mall, Jacksonville's first indoor shopping mall. In addition to a large auditorium, the new facility will house social services, incubating businesses, and retail stores. In 1999, because of his proficiency in economic development, Bishop McLaughlin was named Entrepreneur of the Year by Florida State University.

"If you picked up and left, how would the city feel? Would your city weep? Would anybody even notice? Would anybody care?"

The Multiplex also began and houses a Christian academy attended by five hundred students. The campus includes a dozen state-of-the-art basketball courts that attract young people from all over West Jacksonville for midnight basketball. In addition to economic empowerment and education, they support a prison and jail ministry, a nursing home ministry, a youth ministry, Big and Little Brothers, and free car-repair services. They also have a team of 250 volunteers who "look after things in the city," even if that means simply sweeping the streets of Jacksonville.

Bishop Vaughn McLaughlin is an outstanding preacher, but he believes that ministry is always what happens outside the church. In his words, "If you are not making an impact outside of your four walls, then you are not making an impact at all." He challenges those he mentors by asking them, "If you picked up and left, how would the city feel? Would your city weep? Would anybody even notice? Would anybody care?"[7]

Something to **Think** About

"If you picked up and left, how would the city feel? Would your city weep? Would anybody even notice? Would anybody care?"

Something to **Talk** About

1. Where is your church on the Micah 6:8 blueprint? What percentage of your congregation is involved in each column?

Walk Humbly With God	Love Mercy	Act Justly

Addresses the spiritual lives of those who come to church
• Personal salvation
• Spiritual disciplines
• Seeking the Lord
• Worship
• Becoming a devoted follower
	Addresses individual symptoms of those outside the church
	• Acts of kindness
	• Giving people "fish"
	  Shelter
	  Groceries
	  Clothing
	  Medical care
		Addresses causes that create symptoms
		• Teaching people how to fish and how to own the pond
		  Evangelism/discipleship
		  Tutoring/mentoring
		  Job training
		  Job/business creation
		  Livable wages
		  Home ownership

% Engaged Here	**% Engaged Here**	**% Engaged Here**

2. What specific opportunities to demonstrate mercy and act justly are available to your church?

Something to **Act** Upon

What can you do to get started?

Sermon/**Lesson** Idea

Text: Micah 6:8

Main Idea: God desires all Christians to walk humbly with him, to love mercy, and to act justly. In addition to relying on him, God asks that we move outside ourselves and outside the church to extend mercy and justice to the community.

Illustration: Giving names to people in need of mercy and justice

Action Point: Identify opportunities for your church to demonstrate mercy and act justly within your community.

Endnotes

1. www.quotationspage.com
2. Jack Jezreel, comments (Boulder, CO: speech during a seminar at Sacred Heart of Jesus Catholic Church, December 16, 2002).
3. Harvie M. Conn, *A Clarified Vision for Urban Mission* (Grand Rapids, MI: Zondervan, 1987), 147.
4. Eli Morris, comments (Cordova, TN: interview at Hope Presbyterian Church, March 8, 2002).
5. Luis A. Cortés Jr., comments (Philadelphia, PA: interview at Nueva Esperanza, August 7, 2001).
6. Adolf Harnack, *The Expansion of Christianity in the First Three Centuries, vol. 1* (Eugene, OR: Wipf and Stock Publishers, 1998), 219.
7. Vaughn McLaughlin, comments (Jacksonville, FL: interview at the Potter's House, May 16, 2001).

chapter eight

Casting
the **Vision**

"And no one after drinking old wine wants the new, for he says, 'The old is better.'"
—**Luke 5:39**

Accustomed to Bad Vision

Recently my (Rick's) daughter went to the optometrist for a check-up. That night she said, "I can see so much better!" And it wasn't a new prescription that had helped her; the doctor had discovered that at some point she had inadvertently switched contact lenses, putting the lens intended for her right eye in the left, and vice versa. Though the prescriptions for each contact aren't far apart, they are different. I asked her, "Didn't that bother you?"

She responded, "A little bit, but after a while I kind of got used to it."

That's how it goes, isn't it? We know things aren't quite right. The way the world looks, the way we are approaching things, is just a bit off. But after a while, we get used to seeing the world that way. We learn to live with it and then become accustomed to it. After a while we think of it as normal. We begin to think that is the way things are supposed to be. But God invites us to see the world the way he sees it, to wear his lenses, to see through his eyes. When we do, a lot of things are cleared up.

Beginning a ministry or increasing the scope of an existing ministry is tough. This is always true when you want to accomplish something significant for the kingdom. It's much easier, much more comfortable, much less stressful to sit back and do nothing, but that's not the life God has called us to.

Becoming an externally focused church is not easy. There will be plenty of naysayers who resist *any* change in the church. But it all begins with a vision and a champion. You may have been given that vision, and you may be its champion. It all begins with the vision.

Remember Proverbs 16:9

I have hung my hat on Proverbs 16:9: "In his heart a man plans his course, but the Lord determines his steps." This verse describes exactly how God has worked in my life to provide direction. God has gifted all of us with the ability to think, dream, plan, and counsel. There have been times when I've tried to do all of it: choose a direction, make my plans, set my course, determine my steps—asking God only

Going faster in the wrong direction is never the right answer.

to nudge into place the pieces that were beyond me. I completely ignored the second half of the equation: "The Lord determines his steps." There have also been times when I prayed and did nothing as I waited for God to send me the plan. In doing so, I ignored the first half of the equation: "In his heart a man plans his course."

As you start planning your course, use everything at your disposal to determine how, when, where, and why God might use you in your current situation to be of influence for him. Then pray earnestly, diligently, and passionately that he will direct your steps. Choose a path and pursue it, while remaining attentive to the direction the Father gives.

All Leaders Are Visionaries

True to my gender, I hate to stop and ask for directions. But as I get older, I'm softening a bit and realizing that going faster in the wrong direction is never the right answer. Leaders constantly ask, "Where are we headed and why?"

It is a myth that not all leaders are visionaries. If you lead, you are a visionary. You are inviting people to move from the present to the future. If you don't have any idea of where your church is going and why, then you are not a leader—period. And all leaders, to be successful, must think about their vision for their organization every day.

What Is Vision?

You're probably familiar with the scene in *Alice's Adventures in Wonderland* in which Alice is wandering around, trying to find a way out of Wonderland. She comes to a fork in the road and meets the Cheshire Cat. Alice asks the cat, "Would you tell me, please, which way I ought to go from here?"

"That depends a good deal on where you want to get to," replies the cat.

"I don't much care..." says Alice.

I love the cat's response: "Then it doesn't matter which way you go."

If you were asked right now to explain what your work is about, where it's going, and what you hope happens, could you answer? More important, could you answer in less than five minutes?

Vision is a desirable picture of a future state. Vision informs others what they are exchanging their lives and time for. Vision is like the North Star—a point of reference that guides and directs, but is not necessarily a destination. The authors of *Flight of the Buffalo* write, "Vision is the beginning point for leading the journey. Vision focuses. Vision inspires...Vision is our alarm clock in the morning, our caffeine in the evening. Vision touches the heart. It becomes the criterion against which all behavior is measured...The focus on vision disciplines us to think strategically."[1] Vision is the picture in your mind of what could be and what you hope will be.

God himself is a vision caster. One night he took Abraham "outside and said, 'Look up at the heavens and count the stars—if indeed you can count them.' Then he said to him, 'So shall your offspring be' " (Genesis 15:5). Talk about vision! This compelling picture of the future guided all of Abraham's life.

God gave Joseph a dream for his life when Joseph was seventeen. Though it took twenty-two years for this vision to reach fruition, it nonetheless guided every step of Joseph's life, from how he responded to the lascivious advances of Potiphar's wife, to how he served in Pharaoh's court.

Jesus was a vision caster. He rarely missed an opportunity to let people know what he was about. He had come "to seek and to save what was lost" (Luke 19:10) and "to serve and to give his life as a ransom for many" (Matthew 20:28).

I used to teach that vision is a clear, compelling, magnetic image of a preferable future. (I taught that because I had heard it somewhere, and it sounded good.) Then I got involved in actually leading. Since then I've discov-

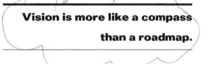

Vision is more like a compass than a roadmap.

ered that vision is more like a compass than a roadmap. It provides direction; it guides; it motivates toward a desirable future.

As you pursue your vision, it takes on a more definite shape. As I prayed for and planned ways to reach our community, it became clear that this would be done through building authentic relationships. As I continued to focus my efforts, I realized that the best way to build relationships is through service. As possibilities turn into realities, more ideas fly through my mind, and I catch a greater glimpse of the vision, and it becomes easier and easier to describe.

As leaders, our job is to communicate the vision and to find ways for others to embrace it. Most people have a difficult time seeing things that aren't already in place. We have to find ways to help them see what we have already seen. For me, sharing the vision happens in our weekly staff meetings; it happens with volunteers and staff over shared meals; it happens when we actually get involved in the things we are describing.

For a vision to attract volunteers and resources, it must be compelling. The following is Vineyard Community Church of Cincinnati's vision statement:

> Imagine a ragtag collection of surrendered and transformed people who love God and others. They are mesmerized by the idea that this is not about them, but all about Jesus. They are transfixed by His story and His heart for their city.

> They are seedthrowers and firestarters, hope peddlers and grace-givers, risktakers and dreamers, young and old. They link arms with anyone who tells the story of Jesus. They empower the poor, strengthen the weak, embrace the outcast, seek the lost. They serve together, play together,

worship together, live life together. Their city will change because God sent them.

They are us.

We believe that small things done with great love will change the world.[2]

Does this vision grab you? Do you find yourself saying, "Don't leave me out! How can I get involved?" Vision casters are storytellers. Vision casters paint pictures with compelling language.

Laurie Beshore, pastor of Lighthouse Ministries of Mariners Church, says:

The last sentence of our vision statement is "We envision a time when those who have nothing will worship and serve beside those who have much, each recognizing that their worth and significance can be found in Christ alone." For us, what begins as ministry becomes family.

One of our businessmen who works a lot with motel families had a birthday party at his home. In this mix were members of YPO (Young Presidents Organization) along with motel families (families who reside in motels year-round). Motel children were running around and playing with the children of the YPOs. The motel kids were comfortable because they had been in this man's home many times before. When I think of what would make God smile…what would bring delight to his eyes, this is the picture I see—that in God's household, rich and poor, we are all family. [3]

As you go forward, describe your vision in such compelling terms that your people will eagerly follow.

Vision Problems

At the same time, bear in mind some of the vision problems common among leaders. Mark Scott, academic dean at Ozark Christian College in Joplin, Missouri, describes some of them:

Nearsighted—These leaders are so focused on the daily stuff and the issues at hand that they can't see things in the distance. Their heads are down, so it's hard for them to see beyond current circumstances.

Farsighted—These leaders are concentrating so hard on the future that they miss the present realities of their situations. They spend so much time envisioning that nothing gets done toward accomplishing the vision.

Tunnel Vision—These leaders are so focused on their situations, issues, and agendas that they miss out on what is happening around them. Far too often in the church this has created a fortress mentality.

Walleyed—While watching the culture and trends, these leaders get all caught up in the latest and greatest. Without much thought or application to their specific situations, they copy the latest fad.

Lazy eye—These leaders may have great vision, but their lack of commitment and effort leads to results that are at best mediocre.[4]

Turning Vision Into Reality

There's a big difference between visionaries and dreamers. Dreamers have an idea a minute and wonderful plans but never seem to put feet to their dreams. An effective leader spends part of every day focused on turning the vision into reality.

To do this, a leader spends time asking these questions: "Who are we? What is the scope of what we do? What are our current competencies? What are our resources? Whom do we serve?" These questions help clarify and define the vision.

It is one thing to say we want to go to the moon, but if we don't have the time, money, or rocket scientists, we aren't likely to get there. We must constantly ask, "What will it take to get to our destination? What competencies need to be developed? What staff should we hire? What resources are needed?"

In your efforts to become externally focused, evaluate the tools and strategies currently in place that will help you move in that direction. Ask yourself, "How can we gain a better understanding of our community and its needs? What are our congregation's strengths and weaknesses? What additional resources do we need? What barriers do we need to overcome? What opportunities could we be involved in right away?"

It is one thing to dream; it is quite another to see those dreams become reality. The effective leader spends a little bit of time every day focused on ways to put feet to the vision.

Ensuring the Vision's Long Life

None of us will lead forever. Effective leaders spend a bit of every day thinking about who will cast the vision after they are gone—thinking about succession. They spend time equipping others for service, especially for leadership. John Maxwell said, "There is only one thing worse than equipping people and losing them; it is not equipping them and keeping them."[5]

For too many ministers, it is easier to be a one-man band. Some of us even wear the label proudly. We may accomplish much, we may stay very busy and be very needed, but we will have failed miserably if we don't bring others along who will carry the vision even further into the future.

Leadership development should be an ongoing part of your responsibilities, not something you put off until a later time. *Ten years* before his retirement, Jack Welch, the former CEO of General Electric, said, "From now on, choosing my successor is the most important decision I'll make. It occupies a considerable amount of thought almost every day."[6]

"Serve Us" and "Service"

Marion Patillo is the executive director of a ministry in Dallas called Metro-Link. Metro-Link serves as a conduit between volunteers from some forty churches in twenty-seven city blocks in South Dallas. Marion observes that when Metro-Link began, there were 955 churches in South Dallas, yet the area was rife with crime, alcoholism, drug addiction, and prostitution. Why? It was certainly not from a lack of churches! The problem centered on the fact that most churches had not been serving the community. Marion says, "Most churches are about 'Serve us!' rather than 'service.' " The first perspective reflects an internal focus: "Help make me be a better person." The second perspective is directed outwardly: "Help me make this world a better place!"

But there is no evidence in the Bible to suggest that discipling, nurturing, and caring for the people already in the church *and* doing whatever is necessary to reach lost people outside the church are mutually exclusive goals. Externally focused churches believe both perspectives are necessary, and that people within the church are best served when they are engaged in service outside the church.

Cars move forward when there is tension between the tires and the pavement. The best drivers know how to manage that tension: when to use the gas, when to apply the brakes, how to navigate the road, how to adjust for prevailing conditions. In the same way, church leaders who would move their churches toward a greater external focus must learn how to manage the dynamic tension between "serve us" and "service."

The Bigger Picture

Embracing the vision of being an externally focused church is more than creating a ministry or task force to decide how or what should be done. Being an externally focused church means helping the Christians in your church see in a new way. It is about encouraging them to see their world, workplace, and neighborhood as places in which to demonstrate God's love. It is about helping to open their eyes to the opportunities around them.

An external focus is not a tactic or a strategy. It is a transformation. It moves people into the heart of the matter—loving and serving.

A Closer Look

Is Service a Tactic or Is It Who You Are?

At one time, LifeBridge Christian Church was structured along fairly traditional lines. We had departments for ministering to youth, children, seniors, and young adults. Often these departments would reflect the passions and giftedness of their leaders, without any guarantee that the church's core values—outreach, spiritual development, worship, and involvement—were equally balanced in each ministry area.

Because we wanted those values to be reflected across the board, in every facet of our ministry, we have since structured ourselves around these four emphasis ministries: outreach (which includes evangelism, community outreach, and missions), spiritual development, worship, and involvement. This has helped to provide content and ideas across the board and has ensured that each is, indeed, emphasized in every facet of ministry. As a result, each ministry department develops plans, events, and activities that reflect our values. For example, the student ministry reflects the distinct passions and gifts of those leading student ministry, but it also reflects our overall mission and vision in every area of its programming.

For our congregation, an external focus isn't the responsibility of one department. There isn't a specific budget line allocated for community impact. We see community outreach as an important part of our overall mission. So each ministry department is encouraged to find ways to make community outreach a part of its programming and plans. For example, our women's ministry looks for ways to get engaged with the Mother House, a home for single moms. This ministry will be helping with remodeling projects, providing supplies and gifts, and creating mentoring relationships. In addition, the women's ministry will be providing gift bags for 150 of the chronically mentally ill in Boulder County. These efforts are as important to the women's ministry as making sure that Bible study and worship opportunities are created for the women of our congregation.

This approach has been vital in helping us create a churchwide culture of community service and outreach. A review of all the ministries of LifeBridge and their use of resources would reflect a heart for those things we say we treasure: outreach, spiritual development, worship, and involvement.

Privilege and Challenge

Leadership is a wonderful privilege as well as a daunting challenge. To capture a vision from the Lord and communicate it to others, to invite others on a journey toward significance and spiritual rewards, to discover that present circumstances, though dark, are opportunities leading to a brighter future, and to plan our ways and invite God to direct our steps—these are amazing gifts.

Joel Barker defines a leader as "someone you would follow to a place you would not go by yourself."[7] Most people today are looking for leadership, longing for someone to show them the places they wouldn't go by themselves. When we lead we are not guaranteed success, we are not promised an easy path, nor are we likely to choose the right road every time. We are, however, invited to lead. Theodore Roosevelt said this:

> It is not the critic who counts: not the man who points out how the strong man stumbles or where the doer of deeds could have done them better. The

credit belongs to the man who is actually in the arena; whose face is marred by dust and sweat and blood; who strives valiantly; who errs and comes up short again and again, because there is no effort without error or short-coming; but who knows the great enthusiasms, the great devotions; who spends himself for a worthy cause; who, at the best, knows, in the end, the triumph of high achievement; and who, at the worst, if he fails, at least he fails while daring greatly, so that his place shall never be with those cold and timid souls who knew neither victory nor defeat.[8]

A Chinese proverb says "If we keep heading in the same direction, we are likely to get where we are headed." If we look down the road and we don't like where it is taking us, why are we heading down that road? If we could look into the future ten, twenty, even fifty years from now, what will our communities look like? What will our congregations look like? Will our community of believers have had any impact on the direction and condition of our communities?

Maybe today would be a good time to stop and ask for directions. More than likely, there's a host of people who would follow if they were convinced you knew where you were going.

Something to **Think** About

"In his heart a man plans his course, but the Lord determines his steps."
—Proverbs 16:9

Something to **Talk** About

1. What is your vision for your ministry? How do you see your plans unfolding?

2. What will it take to realize those plans? How has God affected the process of developing them?

3. Most people today are looking for leadership, longing for someone to show them the places they wouldn't go by themselves. Are you willing to show the way?

Something to **Act** Upon

Choose a path and pursue it, while remaining attentive to the direction the Father gives.

Sermon/**Lesson** Idea

Text: Isaiah 32:8

Main Idea: Great vision is often communicated through noble people.
1. If you want to make a difference, be a noble person.
   • A noble person isn't described directly, but the fool (verses 5-7) is described in contrast.
2. If you want to make a difference, make noble plans.
   • Dream great dreams.
3. If you want to make a difference, do noble deeds.
   • Discover your gifts and abilities and those of your congregation.

Illustration: True nobility is defined by service not position. Contrast Mother Teresa and Princess Diana.

Action Point: Assess the needs of your community, and invite others to join you in serving God by meeting those needs.

Endnotes

1. James A. Belasco and Ralph C. Stayer, *Flight of the Buffalo* (New York: Warner Books, 1993), 90.
2. From the www.cincyvineyard.com Web site. Used with permission.
3. Laurie Beshore, comments (Dallas, TX: message, May 28, 2003).
4. Mark Scott, comments (Longmont, CO: seminar at LifeBridge Community Church, 1998). Used with permission.
5. John Maxwell, comments (San Diego, CA: Mega Church Conference, February, 2002).
6. http://w3.hcgnet.com/succession_main.html
7. Joel Barker, *Leadershift,* a training video offered by Employee University.
8. Theodore Roosevelt, "Citizenship in a Republic," a speech delivered at the Sorbonne, Paris, April 23, 1910.

chapter nine

Assessing the **Needs** of Your **Community**

"Philosophers only interpret the world; the point remains to change it."

—Karl Marx

Open Your Eyes

"What? What do you mean, we have to go through Samaria? We don't have to go through Samaria! We can go around Samaria and still get to Galilee. You know, Lord, sometimes slower and longer end up being faster." Jesus just smiled. They would go through Samaria...that country sandwiched between Judea and Galilee. The Samaritans were those who had compromised their Jewish heritage by intermarrying with their foreign captors when the Assyrians had conquered Jerusalem. For over four hundred years, the rift between the Jews and Samaritans had grown wider. The Samaritans were the "compromisers," the half-breed Jews who had sold out. It was suspected that just as they had mixed their marriages, they had also mixed their religions. Following the traditions of their fathers, the Samaritans looked to Mount Gerizim as their spiritual fount, while the Jews looked to the holy city of Jerusalem. For many valid reasons, "Jews [did] not associate with Samaritans" (John 4:9). But Jesus did.

Jesus and the disciples came to a town called Sychar. It was noon and time for lunch. With a bit of trepidation, the disciples went into town to buy food while Jesus rested by the well outside of town. It was an uncomfortable situation. They had never been in this neighborhood before. They completed their task and returned to find Jesus talking with a woman as he rested at the well. The woman went back to the city. Then she returned and brought with her many Samaritans. As they were approaching, Jesus said to his disciples, "I tell you, open your eyes and look at the fields! They are ripe for harvest" (John 4:35).

Most likely their eyes were already physically open, but he wanted them to understand what they were seeing. It wasn't about vision; it was about understanding. The Samaritans were not the enemy; they were potential followers of Jesus. Sometimes as we focus on ourselves, our inadequacies, and our fears, we miss opportunities for ministry. Strange neighborhoods conjure up fear, not compassion. But if we are in ministry, we need to change our focus and realize it's not about us…it's about them.

What Could We Do?

How can your church engage in the needs and dreams of your community? Where can you serve? What opportunities lie before you that your church can embrace? The course of Nehemiah's life was changed when he understood the implications of his brother's report on the condition of the city of Jerusalem: The people "are in great trouble and disgrace. The wall of Jerusalem is broken down, and its gates have been burned with fire" (Nehemiah 1:1-3). Nehemiah's burden to transform the city (Nehemiah 1–7) and transform the people (Nehemiah 8–13) came from accurate information. He changed the course of his life based on accurate and compelling information. As your church develops an external focus, here are several suggestions for uncovering the information needed for potential ministry opportunities.

First, ask the people you are serving to identify their needs and dreams. Rather than assuming what they need, let them tell you. Mariners

Church volunteers began to meet with the residents of an underserved Latino community in Santa Ana. Through a translator they asked, "What is it you want for your neighborhood?" After hours of talking and listening, their neighbors identified three paramount needs:

1. They needed help keeping their kids in school. The dropout rate in this community is among the highest in the nation, and without education, cycles of poverty continue. The parents expressed their limited ability to help their children because of their own lack of education and lack of proficiency in the English language.

2. They needed help in improving their parenting skills.

3. They needed instruction in English so they could get better jobs.

To bear fruit, compassion must give birth to strategy. So the folks at Mariners developed the Minnie Street Learning Center in Santa Ana and based its curriculum on these three needs.

In the spring of 2003, the pastoral staff of Desert Springs Bible Church in Phoenix invited the principal of a local elementary school to address the congregation during the Sunday morning services. The principal shared the needs and dreams of his under-resourced school and invited the congregation to step in and help. Two hundred people responded by "adopting" three grades of the elementary school by providing help with school supplies as well as classroom tutoring. They looked to the community to inform them of the needs, and they looked to God to inform them of his solutions.

To bear fruit, compassion must give birth to strategy.

Second, conduct or use existing research on the needs and dreams of your community. It is often not necessary for churches to do the research themselves because much of it has already been done. For example, formal census research can be found under http://factfinder.census.gov/. Navigating around your zip code will reveal the latest information regarding income and educational levels, demographics, and employment statistics. This is a great start in understanding a community's needs. Your local chamber of commerce is also a good source of valuable information. In 2000 our own county, through the hard work of the Boulder County Civic Forum, spent thousands of hours and dollars identifying the county's assets and its greatest needs and published the results in a report titled "Quality of Life in Boulder County: A Community Indicators Report." We've found this information to be invaluable in understanding the needs and dreams of our community. (You may download a copy from www.bococivicforum.org.)

Because no such document existed in Little Rock, Arkansas, Fellowship Bible Church paid for an outside research group "to objectively identify the most significant social needs and problems that impact the 'quality of life' in Pulaski County and to describe how well the faith community is equipped to meet and respond to those needs." The survey identified such issues as race

> **Research serves as a road map for bringing the life and love of the church to the needs and pains of the community.**

relations, education, youth in poverty, housing, violence, and health care. This kind of research serves as a road map for bringing the life and love of the church to the needs and pains of the community.

Do organizations exist in your community that already do some of the legwork and screening that you need in order to get started in volunteering? While brainstorming ideas for a new campus, LifeBridge Christian Church discovered the St. Vrain Community Council (described in detail in Chapter 2) and began attending its meetings. Through this organization, the LifeBridge team learned what agencies exist, what they do, and how LifeBridge can help to support them. Most communities have an organized method for nonprofits to share ideas and projects.

As the vision to become more externally focused developed from concept to concrete service opportunities, LifeBridge formed a Community Outreach Advisory team. Its goal is to establish meaningful relationships with local nonprofits for the purpose of serving with them. One such relationship is with the Volunteer Connection, a gold mine of community-service information and opportunities.

The Volunteer Connection is a clearinghouse for community groups and other nonprofits to find volunteers. Through the developing relationship between LifeBridge and the Volunteer Connection, LifeBridge has been able to place several Christian volunteers in non-Christian environments to serve.

Each week, the church advertises the Volunteer Connection's volunteer opportunities in the LifeBridge newsletter. This helps the people of the church stay informed about volunteer opportunities in the community.

A Closer Look

The Volunteer Connection

Established in 1969 as a division of the United Way, the Volunteer Connection was one of the first volunteer information and referral centers in the nation. Its mission is to "promote volunteerism, connect volunteers with opportunities, and help organizations effectively engage volunteers to meet community needs." They annually refer thousands of families, individuals, youth, businesses, and corporate and service groups to over 450 agencies and governmental programs in need of volunteers. They also offer workshops, conferences, and consulting services on volunteer management; provide referral counseling services, free of charge, to help assess volunteer interests and skills; and maintain a database of volunteer positions.

This organization helps identify service projects appropriate for faith-based organizations and service clubs, taking into account organizational interests and values. It sometimes helps establish collaborative work projects with like-minded organizations. Projects may be short- or long-term and support a wide variety of skill levels and interests.

Funding for this organization comes from many sources throughout the community, including government grants (47 percent); contracts from businesses for employee volunteer programs (41 percent); and contributions, foundations, grants, and fundraisers (12 percent).[1]

Third, recognize the power of existing relationships. To identify ministry opportunities, look through the eyes of those in your church. Often you will already have a "champion" who, not in conjunction with the church, is leading a ministry. A motivated leader is worth his or her weight in gold, forming a one-person nucleus around which to build a team. Look for places where God is already at work through good-hearted people, and ask if you can join in.

Most likely your church also has its share of "professionals"—people who possess an enhanced awareness of community needs because of their jobs. Though they may not realize it, police officers, social workers, non-profit board members, schoolteachers, and school administrators are all experts in identifying the community's needs. Forming a working group or task force with these people would put you well on the way toward identifying multiple ministry opportunities.

During several evenings of brainstorming, the people of LifeBridge identified over five thousand ways they could serve their community. Who within your church knows a lot about your community? Look around at your congregation. You are likely to find a number of people who are already plugged into various groups and can provide guidance and open doors for involvement. Find out what they know. Learn the system.

A Closer Look

The Community Outreach Team
at LifeBridge Christian Church

This team provides direction and guidance to the church's ministry programs. It is made up of several schoolteachers and businessmen, an office manager at a doctor's office, and occasionally the ministry staff. What do these people have in common? They are all civic minded, and they know the system or have been excited about learning the system. They help sort through the myriad of community service opportunities, assess the needs of organizations, and determine how LifeBridge can be a part of meeting those needs. In essence, they do all the preliminary work of determining the who, what, when, where, and how of community impact. Then they work with a ministry program (such as men's, children's, and students') to determine how the church can meet the need. The team also helps decide who will provide the leadership for each opportunity. Here's an example of how it works:

A local community group asks LifeBridge to help provide maintenance for transitional housing. The Community Outreach Team appoints one of its own to explore the possibility and the expectations. Once these are defined and the group decides this is something we can and should do, they meet with one or more ministry areas to determine how to proceed. In this case, the men's ministry will take on the project and will determine how best to recruit volunteers and provide the maintenance needs. The point person from Community Outreach is a liaison between the church and the community group until a relationship is created between the community group and its coordinator from men's ministry.

Another ministry area may partner with men's ministry to accomplish the task, but only one ministry area will take the lead for the project. In this way, community outreach isn't simply a department in the church that recruits like-minded people and finds ways to get involved. Community outreach is a mind-set for *all* ministry areas, and the Community Outreach Team serves as traffic coordinator.

Fourth, look and listen. An important means of assessing needs and opportunities is simply through personal observation. How do we know the needs and dreams of a city? "Ears that hear and eyes that see—the Lord has made them both" (Proverbs 20:12).

A Closer Look

The Dream Center

In 1994, twenty-one-year-old pastor Matthew Barnett began the Dream Center in Los Angeles by walking around his neighborhood, looking for unmet needs. He saw thousands of outcast people living on the fringes of society. Today the Dream Center—"the church that never sleeps"—has adopted fifty city blocks (twenty-one hundred homes!) that it serves with two hundred volunteer staff. Its campus, a former hospital, houses four hundred people in its rehab and discipleship program and feeds more than twenty-five thousand people a week. They have a wellness clinic, a mobile medical unit, and dozens of other effective ministries that are finding needs and meeting them. Their forty buses bring hundreds of people to this church in downtown Los Angeles. What began with personal observation is resulting in changed lives as dozens come to faith each week. Scores of churches around our country have also established an Adopt-a-Block strategy as a means of touching the lives of people around them.

Nearly every day, newspapers report budget cuts in human-service agencies or describe other events that provide new opportunities for the church. When we read in the morning paper that poverty rose for a second straight year and that 1.7 million more people have dropped below the poverty line, we should realize that this means there are 1.7 million more opportunities for the church than there were last year. Every downturn in the economy provides new opportunities for the church to serve.

A Closer Look

9/11

In November 2001, my wife, Diane, and I (Rick) were in New York City assisting with some of the ongoing relief efforts coordinated through the Orchard Group, a church-planting organization in New York. This group collected over $1 million to support relief efforts.

LifeBridge Christian Church was the second highest contributor to this fund, and we were invited to assist with some of the distribution efforts. The first wave of money was given directly to families who had lost loved ones. Diane and I had the privilege of participating in the second wave of distribution to the small businesses in and around the World Trade Center. It was hard to believe that many people were still trying to survive at "ground zero" in the weeks following the tragedy.

While we knew the amounts we were giving (generally $2,500 per business and no more than $500 per employee) were just drops in the bucket compared to the need, the money provided immediate help when it was desperately needed. One New York Times reporter stated, "There have been plenty of groups down here passing out brochures but nobody passing out cash."

That same reporter asked the members of Orchard Group why they had chosen to give to small businesses. "There were thousands of people whose only livelihood was from these businesses. Most didn't have insurance to cover the loss of being closed for six to nine weeks, and most of these small businesses derived their income from the traffic at the WTC," a member of Orchard Group replied. While a process exists for receiving government aid, it is often tedious and many times provides no more than $1,000.

It was a moving experience. Beyond seeing the devastation of the WTC, we experienced the raw emotion of those who had seen the attacks, watched the buildings fall, and lost friends and co-workers. Many couldn't remove the images from their minds. Diane and I went from store to store asking for the owner or manager. Most of the places had just re-opened but were discovering that there was not much business. We told them that Christians around the country had collected money in order to help. Some would tell us that they weren't Christians. We responded, "That isn't a criterion." Others would ask what strings were attached. We said, "None." Some cried; others were stunned. One even called us angels. One response was universal: They all wanted to tell the story of what they'd seen and how it had changed them.

We went to New York to be a blessing and came home feeling blessed. Even now, Diane and I still get a Christmas card each year from Mrs. Kim, one of the small-business owners we met in 2001. Maybe the generosity of Christians spoke a simple message of love and made an impression of Christ on someone's heart.

Some churches provide "micro-journeys" for teams of people to personally investigate the needs and ministry opportunities of a city. Pastor Eli Morris of Hope Presbyterian Church near Memphis has been offering "urban plunges" to anyone God invites to consider the underserved of the community—the widow, the orphan, the alien, the poor, the elderly, the children, the prisoners, the sick, and the disabled.

Dr. Raymond Bakke suggests that the needs of these folks can be classified into six categories:

- physical needs
- spiritual/moral needs
- social/relational needs
- emotional needs
- educational needs
- training/mentoring needs

He goes on to demonstrate how to chart the opportunities, based on the types of people in need and their types of needs. See the partially completed chart below for an example.[2]

	The Poor	Children	The Aged	Widows/ Single Parents	Orphans	Prisoners	The Sick/the Disabled	Aliens/ Immigrants
Physical	Medical care	Flu shots, backpacks	Meal delivery	Lawns mowed, home repairs	School clothes	Birthday cards for children	Wheelchairs	Food, clothing, shelter
Spiritual	To feel welcome in church	Basic spiritual instruction	Church services in nursing homes	Small groups for single parents and widows	Ride to church or youth group	Hope, restoration, forgiveness	Prayer	Connection with believers
Social	Connected with others in the community	To be in safe, healthy environments	Companion-ship: someone to listen	Companion-ship: someone to listen	Big brother/ big sister	Visitation, watching out for prisoners' children	Care	Welcome into life of community
Emotional								
Educational								
Vocational								

One way of identifying service opportunities in your community is to give one of these grids to each of your church's small groups and ask them to drive around town, read the newspapers, talk to people in the neighborhood, and so forth to identify needs. When the grid is completed, each small group will have identified over forty ministry opportunities. Now you're well on your way to answering the question "What could we do?"

What Should We Do?

As you narrow your focus from "What could we do?" to "What should we do?" you will begin to evaluate your church's individual strengths and capacities. You can't do everything, nor should you try. Your opportunities should be broad enough to engage the passions of all of your church members but focused enough to be achievable. Remember that the magnitude and type of service opportunities will be different in every community. Ask the people in your church what they are passionate about. What common thread runs through all of your current ministries? It might be "youth" or "the poor" or "single moms." Focus on what you do well.

You can't do everything, nor should you try.

Whatever your focus, aim for the double benefit of changing the lives of those who are serving as well as of those who are being served.

What Will We Do?

After your church has decided what it should do, develop a concise statement of your mission (what you do), your vision (what you hope to accomplish), and those you serve and minister to. A mission statement is not a spice cabinet of good intentions. A mission statement declares to the world what you want to be held accountable for. But don't wait for the perfectly worded document before you begin. The more you actually do, the clearer your mission and vision will become.

A mission statement is not a spice cabinet of good intentions.

"What you should do" is an imperative that can be backed up with Scriptures and forms the supporting columns of your externally focused mission statement. For example, before the people of Mariners Church began their

Lighthouse Ministries project several years ago, they spent one year studying every Scripture that related to God's heart for the needs of the community. They emerged from this yearlong project with the values that guide all that they do. Their central verse is Jeremiah 22:16: "He defended the cause of the poor and needy, and so all went well. Is that not what it means to know me?" This passage gave birth to the mission of Lighthouse Ministries: "serving people who are poor and in need in our community so that all may experience the transforming power of God's love," and their poignant vision:

> We seek to build a community that values compassion, generosity and humility above power, wealth and prestige. We envision a time when those who have nothing will worship and serve beside those who have much, each recognizing that their worth and significance can be found in Christ alone.[3]

Most likely you will discover more opportunities than you have the capacity to fulfill. Here are some ideas for narrowing your selections. First, you may want to draw a geographical radius around the church in terms of miles or driving time. Second, establish some "engagement criteria" that can be applied to every opportunity. These are the things that matter most to your church. In this process, consider asking these questions (and others more specific to your particular situation):

1. Does this opportunity put us in relationship with those we seek to help or alongside others who are serving?

2. Is this ministry or agency willing to work with us as a faith-based organization?

3. Will this ministry or agency allow us to minister holistically—not just meeting physical needs but spiritual and social needs as well?

4. Do we have people who are ready, willing, and able to develop this ministry?

5. Will this opportunity result in changed lives?

Eventually all visions and missions must come down to real work being done by actual people in real time. Who will do what, by when? Work plans need to be developed and accountability issues need to be discussed. How will you measure what you do? The following chart may be a helpful template in designing a work plan.

Ministry Goal	Desired Outcome	As Measured by...	Action Steps	Team Leader	Completed by...

How Well Do You See?

How do you see your community? It's possible that we see only the things that are wrong and how muddy the water has gotten. We may not like the direction in which things are going or the people who are taking them that way. A convicting scene in Scripture is in Luke 7. Jesus is dining with the Pharisee Simon when a woman with a not-so-great reputation begins to wash Jesus' feet. Simon thinks, "If this man were a prophet, he would know who was washing his feet and how bad she is." In verse 44, Jesus says to Simon, "Do you see this woman?" This wasn't an eye test. Simon wasn't in need of glasses. In effect, Jesus was asking, "Do you *see* this woman? Or do you only see what is wrong with her and how she has messed up her life? Can you only see how muddy she has made the water? Simon, do you see, really *see* this woman? Do you see her as I see her; can you see her as the Father sees her? Can you see what could happen if she knew someone credible who could talk to her about grace? Can you see how she isn't all that different from you? How do you *see* the woman?"

If our responsibility is to be fruit producers in the kingdom and to fulfill the Great Commission and the Great Commandment, then we just may have to see our community differently. We need to earn the right to be heard with a message that can heal the holes in people's hearts. Serving provides a bridge that can build those relationships. Through those relationships, we may have the opportunity to share the good news of grace. Can you even begin to imagine what would happen if the people in our churches really *saw* the people around them as Christ sees them?

Something to **Think** About

Rather than assuming what the people in your community need, let them tell you. "Ears that hear and eyes that see—the Lord has made them both" (Proverbs 20:12).

Something to **Talk** About

1. Evaluate the assessment methods suggested in this chapter, and select the ones that make the most sense for your church.

2. Have small groups collect newspaper and news magazine clippings that reflect potential opportunities for the church.

3. Using Dr. Bakke's chart (p. 166), ask small groups to identify the needs of the underserved in your community.

4. Ask city officials about their needs and dreams for the community.

5. Read the newspaper. Bad news for the community may create new opportunities for your church to show the love of Christ.

6. Form groups from your church, and drive around looking for needs and dreams.

7. Look at what God is already doing in the community through common grace, and join in.

8. Choose one or two opportunities and begin!

9. Build on your successes.

Sermon/**Lesson** Idea

Text: Nehemiah 1–13

Main Point: The course of Nehemiah's life was changed when he understood the implications of his brother's report on the condition of the city of Jerusalem (Nehemiah 1:1-3). The people "are in great trouble and disgrace" and "the wall...is broken down, and its gates have been burned with fire."

Nehemiah's burden to transform the city (Nehemiah 1–7) and transform the people (Nehemiah 8–13) came from accurate information. He changed the course of his life based on accurate and compelling information.

Illustration: Pull out copies of the last four or five issues of your local newspaper, and identify needs that the church could begin to meet.

Action Point: Review the suggestions under "Something to Talk About," choose one, and begin.

Endnotes

1. http://bcn.boulder.co.us/vconnect/index.html
2. Raymond Bakke, "Spiritual Resources for Transformational Leadership," a class offered in Seattle, Washington, on June 10, 2002. Used with permission.
3. Mariners Church Lighthouse Ministries Blueprint, 9.

chapter ten

Organizing
for Usefulness

"However beautiful the strategy, you should occasionally look at the results."

—Winston Churchill [1]

Aoccdrnig to rseearch...

In September 2003, a story began circulating on the Internet about supposed "research" done at Cambridge University regarding reading perception. Read the following paragraph to find out what was discovered.

> *Aoccdrnig to rseearch at Cmabrigde Uinervtisy, it deosn't mttaer in waht oredr the ltteers in a wrod are, the olny iprmoatnt tihng is taht the frist and lsat ltteer be at the rghit pclae. The rset can be a total mses and you can sitll raed it wouthit porbelm. Tihs is bcuseae the huamn mnid deos not raed ervey lteter by istlef, but the wrod as a wlohe.*
>
> *Amzanig, huh?*

Whether this "research" was actually conducted or not, if you were able to quickly grasp the meaning of the foregoing paragraph, you get the point—we do focus on patterns of letters more than on individual letters within words.

Sometimes in ministry we assume we need to get everything just so before we can start—that people need to get the whole picture and have complete understanding before they can move forward. But the truth is, all they really need is enough understanding to get started. Part of being externally focused is to build the road as we travel it. We don't need the entire road before we begin the journey, only enough to take the next step.

> **Part of being externally focused is to build the road as we travel it.**

Once you have assessed the needs of the community, how can you turn your vision into a practical organizational structure that will get things done? This chapter addresses the major challenges of giving life to the vision: staffing, funding, building partnerships, and measuring results.

Staffing

There are two primary approaches to staffing for an externally focused church, each with inherent strengths and weaknesses.

Approach 1—The first model has no staff specifically assigned to "community ministry" or "community engagement." Externally focused churches that take this route expect all staff and all areas of ministry to have an externally focused approach to ministry. Each staff member's plan includes ways to love and serve the community. Each staff member recruits volunteers for the projects in which he or she is engaged. The strength of this model is that it forces everyone to think about getting outside the walls of the church. Churches whose external focus is intrinsic to their identities find this to be a useful staffing model.

Approach 2—A second way to promote an external focus is to create a staff position responsible specifically for community engagement or volunteer deployment. The ability to place a full-time staff person in this position is largely based on the resources of the church. As external ministry grows and volunteers are deployed, even more full-time positions may be needed and created.

What are the necessary qualifications for people in this position? First, you need people with big hearts, people who are passionate about community transformation. You cannot delegate passion or buy passion. Second, you need people who have a track record for effectively recruiting and mobilizing capable volunteers.

Paid Volunteers

One of the most innovative ideas in the church-staffing arena is to pay volunteers. *Paid volunteer* may sound like an oxymoron, but the idea actually makes a lot of sense: Select "high-capacity" leaders, and pay them $10,000 a year for ten hours of work each week. Their job is to recruit, train, and deploy ten volunteers, who in turn lead small groups of ten to twelve people apiece. So in essence you are gaining a "pastor" of a congregation of 110 to 130 for a modest $10,000 a year.

Churches employing this model have discovered that in selecting high-capacity leaders, they are buying their best, most passionate ten hours of the week. Normally these high-capacity folks are not working for the money, but because they are paid, they are extremely reliable and will get the job done. In addition, by hiring five people for a total of $50,000 a year, the hiring risks are reduced. If these people are selected well, the chances of all of them washing out are pretty slim.

Keep an Eye Out for "Half-Timers"

A few years ago, Bob Buford, founder of Leadership Network, wrote a best-selling book called *Half-Time: Changing Your Game From Success to Significance*. "Half-timers" are those successful individuals who have achieved many of their goals in life and now are wondering what to do with the rest of their lives. They long to do something significant but are unsure about how to get involved, or they feel awkward doing so. This group may very well be the largest untapped and underutilized resource in the body of Christ. These folks are part of the labor pool that stands around (usually on their boats or on golf courses) because they are seldom asked to take part in the harvest or, if asked, are given responsibilities far below their abilities.

But Whatever You Do...

A few months after Moses was born, his mother put the baby into a basket and placed the basket among the reeds along the bank of the Nile River.

After a short while, the daughter of Pharaoh discovered the baby, pulled the basket from the water, and began searching for a woman among the Hebrews who could nurse him. Moses' mother was brought to the daughter of Pharaoh, where she was told, "Take this baby and nurse him for me, and I will pay you" (Exodus 2:9). Isn't that the grace of God? Moses' mother was paid to do what she was born to do.

When hiring staff, make certain the job and their passions are intertwined, that they are being paid to do something they were born to do. It's too big and too important just to be a job.

Mobilizing the Entire Church

When we speak of volunteers, we are referring to those who are engaging in ministry of any type; they are usually the "unpaid staff" of the church. Volunteering is really the avenue for Christians to be in shoulder-to-shoulder, face-to-face relationships with those who are yet to become Christians. If you are leading volunteers, you know you have a challenging job. Your job (in the paraphrased words of legendary Dallas Cowboys coach Tom Landry) is "to get a group of people to do something they don't want to do, that they might achieve something they have wanted all of their lives."[2] You get to recruit reluctant, fearful, hesitant people—then watch them become fully alive as they learn how to give their lives away to others.

Erwin McManus of Mosaic in Los Angeles takes a unique approach that transforms congregants into ministers. To become a part of Mosaic's community is quite easy. People must simply declare that they "want to be a part of this community of faith." But Erwin challenges everyone in that community to become part of Mosaic's self-supported staff. To be on the staff of Mosaic requires four commitments:

1. to live a holy life (understanding that no one does it perfectly, but to come clean when you fail)
2. to be an active participant in ministry outside the church
3. to be a generous giver, as reflected in tithing
4. to live an evangelistic lifestyle

Over four hundred of the thirteen hundred attending adults at Mosaic have been anointed and commissioned to be part of the church staff. [3] Could your church do the same?

Lowering the Thresholds

Every church that seeks to mobilize 100 percent of its congregation in ministry needs to define the minimum qualifications for a volunteer. These aren't *ideal* qualifications but *minimum* qualifications. In taking a minimalist approach to ministry, we refer to Acts 15, possibly the most important chapter in the book of Acts. Until the Council at Jerusalem, it was unclear whether a Gentile follower of Christ had to become a Jew—undergoing circumcision (if a male) and keeping the ritual and dietary laws—in addition to embracing Jesus. The council did not define everything a person needed to do to grow into Christlikeness. That wasn't the point. The council wanted to fulfill the mission of spreading the gospel. It recognized that requiring believers to adopt the tenets of Judaism in addition to trusting Jesus Christ was a barrier to the entire non-Jewish world. The council wanted to remove the barriers to coming to Christ. After much discussion, the Apostle James said, "It is my judgment...that we should not make it difficult for the Gentiles who are turning to God" (Acts 15:19). [4]

A Closer Look

Saddleback Community Church

As Saddleback Community Church in Lake Forest, California, moved toward getting small groups formed around "Forty Days of Purpose," members of the leadership counted up their "qualified" small-group leaders. The leaders at Saddleback are well aware of the biblical warnings against novices teaching, and so they've required that small-group leaders be skilled in guiding discussion, delving into the Scriptures, and helping people apply the Word to their lives. A count of those who possessed these leadership skills came to three hundred—not nearly enough to accommodate more than fifteen thousand members and regular attendees. But they did have three thousand people who were able to open their homes, serve a few refreshments, and play a video or DVD, while Saddleback leaders provided the content. The threshold was effectively lowered, allowing thousands of people to minister to others.

What are your church's qualifications for its volunteers? Granted, the qualifications (and screening) must be different for people involved in mentoring youth than for people who are building cabinets for the women's shelter. But are the minimum qualifications set at a level that allows everyone who can breathe to qualify for something that will put him or her face to face, shoulder to shoulder with people in the community?

Churches that seek to mobilize every person must also define *ministry* in a broad enough way to encompass the skills, experiences, giftedness, passions, and relationships of every person in the church. We define *ministry* as meeting someone else's needs with the resources God has entrusted to you. Many, many people will never lead a Bible study, but they can still minister to others through the gifts God has entrusted to them. Ministry can be changing oil or doing basic car repair for single moms. Ministry can be teaching handicapped children to ride horses. Once churches expand their definition of *ministry,* the sky is the limit for meaningful opportunities for service.

> Once churches expand their definition of ministry, the sky is the limit for meaningful opportunities for service.

Addressing the need to make opportunities accessible to every member, Dave Workman, senior pastor of Vineyard Community Church in Cincinnati, says, "We want to lower the bar to service to allow all of our people to make meaningful connection to the community."[5] Because the people of Vineyard believe everyone can be a servant, there are many easy-entry, "low-touch, high-grace" events in which members can engage. They range from handing out free soft drinks or smoke detector batteries to cleaning restrooms at the local gas station. To give people a taste for ministry, your church must increase the number and frequency of drop-in, get-your-feet-wet opportunities.

> To give people a taste for ministry, your church must increase the number and frequency of drop-in, get-your-feet-wet opportunities.

We also need to be ready to encourage and empower people to look for opportunities to begin their own ministries. Judy Pitt is a successful realtor in Boulder who possesses a big heart and a keen mind. A few years ago, she began building a relationship with the homeless men selling newspapers at some of the busy intersections in town. Her ministry became known as "On the Corner." It included delivering food and beverages to these men where they stood, unprotected from the elements, as well as having kids from the youth group sell the papers on Sunday mornings so the men could go to church and Sunday school. Today several of these men are pulling their lives together because of the creative way God is working through Judy.

Motivating Volunteers

Churches that are good at recruiting and motivating volunteers have figured out a way to keep them coming back...and enjoying the experience. Dave Workman says, "We have to figure out ways for the volunteers to get 'paid.'" In his case, he doesn't mean paid with cash, but in other ways—ways that are meaningful to the volunteers. What one person considers pay may be meaningless to another person. Pay is whatever motivates people. Some people are motivated by challenge and responsibility, others by affiliation (who they work with and for), others by influence (an opportunity to make a difference), some by self-improvement (personal growth), and still others by enjoyment ("This will really be fun!").

Pay is whatever motivates people.

One thing all potential volunteers need is a clear idea of the need, what their part is in serving that need (how much and for how long), whom they will be working with, and the expected outcome of their involvement. If you want people's hearts, they need to know what they are exchanging their lives for. As you grow and get better organized, job descriptions are a must. Make the job descriptions as useful as possible by asking volunteers to refine them as they learn what the jobs are really about.

Recruiting Volunteers

In your church there are most likely some who volunteer for nearly everything. There is another small percentage of people who will never volunteer, no matter what the opportunity or perceived benefits are. It is the large group in the middle that you should recruit.

Because people are motivated by different factors, you've got to draw from all the clubs in your bag to be an effective recruiter. Tim Keller of Redeemer Presbyterian Church in New York City writes that the process of transforming members into ministers "starts by articulating clearly and regularly a theology of every-member ministry...From the pulpit, in classes, by word of mouth, it must be communicated that *every layperson is a minister*, and that *ministry is finding needs and meeting them with the goal of the spread of the kingship of Christ.*"[6]

In a recent brainstorming session, leaders of externally focused churches identified some practical ways to recruit volunteers. The following is a partial summary of that list:

- Host special events at which volunteers are recognized and appreciated, times that showcase what God is doing through externally focused ministries.

- Tell "God stories"—stories showing how God works through ordinary people to change the lives of others.

- Solicit testimonies from church members.

- Solicit testimonies from people who have benefited from the ministry.

- Recruit the leaders. Let the leaders recruit the team.

- Personally challenge a person to do a specific job for a specific period of time.

- Rotate all volunteer leaders out of leadership after two years. Always have a leader in training.

- Identify a variety of needs and volunteer opportunities.

A Closer Look

Lighthouse Ministries

In the 1980s the people of Mariners Church asked themselves two questions: "What could we do?" and "What should we do?" This was the beginning of the church's Lighthouse Ministries. In 2002 Lighthouse Ministries employed the hearts and entrepreneurial skills of nearly four thousand volunteers to minister to the under-resourced people of Orange County.

These volunteers gave 110,000 hours of service (the equivalent of over fifty full-time staff members!) as they tutored foster children, mentored motel families, took kids to camp, visited the elderly, taught English at one of their learning centers, worked in the car ministry (in 2002 eight cars were given away, and $150,000 was raised to benefit Lighthouse Ministries) or Mariners' thrift store (realizing $168,000 in sales), distributed Christmas gifts, helped teenagers with team building at their leadership camp, assisted with immigration papers, worked in transitional housing, and volunteered with Orange County Social Services.

The people in these ministries view volunteering as simply the avenue to build relationships with people in the community. Each year they celebrate a "lighthouse weekend" in which they share stories of changed lives in the community and the church. They have figured out ways to get thousands of people out into the community by making ministry the normative expression of faith, not just something reserved for the professionals.

Everyone at Mariners is regularly encouraged to serve, with the church providing multiple and frequent "safe first-step" opportunities that anyone can take. Safe first-steps require no screening or training—volunteers can cook hamburgers at camp, help with sports days, or dance with senior citizens at the Mariners' Senior Prom. Safe first-steps require no ongoing commitment. Those who want to go further in their volunteering can be part of ongoing commitments such as tutoring, mentoring, being a "life skills" coach, or working with pregnant teenagers.

Keeping Volunteers

How does a church keep its external focus after the newness has worn off? One important way is to continue to communicate the results of the church's efforts. During the first years of LifeBridge Christian Church's Time to Serve, each service project coordinator was given a disposable camera. The pictures, along with video footage, were used during a church worship service a month later. This accomplished two things. First, it commended those who served and reminded them of their experience, inspiring them to do it again. Second, it showed the folks who were not involved what they had missed. Participation in A Time to Serve at LifeBridge continues to grow each year. And a team of photographers now captures poignant moments of community service all year long.

Developing Leaders

Nothing happens without leadership. Every church that is devoted to a mission will always find itself short of leadership. But leaders don't just drop in. They are developed. If you are responsible for deploying volunteer leaders, what should you do to develop their leadership qualities? If you are a volunteer, what are reasonable expectations for your develop-

> **Trust is one of the highest forms of motivation.**

ment? Sue Mallory, author of *The Equipping Church,* writes, "The church by definition is the greatest gathering of potential servants in the world, but she is also the most notorious vehicle for disappointing, discouraging, and even destroying them. Only a small percentage of willing volunteers can succeed without specific training and clear direction—and the church seldom offers either."[7]

Find a mentor, teacher, judge and cheerleader. We often think our job is done when a volunteer shows up, but that is really only the beginning. Peter Drucker relates a conversation with a pastor of a large church that had become proficient in developing volunteer leaders. "He told me the church tries to provide four things to young people who show up for services: (1) a mentor to guide him or her; (2) a teacher to develop skills; (3) a judge to evaluate progress; and finally, (4) an encourager to cheer them on.[8] In addition to this pastor's sage advice, we would add the following.

Master the art of delegation. The goal of delegation, first of all, is that the person succeeds in accomplishing the job he or she has been given. Failure is seldom a good motivator to take on new and greater responsibilities. The second goal is that the person develops in competence, confidence, and faithfulness. The person who delegates must

- decide what needs to be done.
- select the best person for the job. Let him or her know you believe he or she can do it. Trust is one of the highest forms of motivation.

- clarify and agree upon the desired result and deadline. Concentrate on *what,* not how; *results,* not methodology.

- define guidelines and describe potential pitfalls. Let him or her learn from your mistakes and the mistakes of others.

- establish levels of authority and accountability and a method of evaluation.

- identify financial, human, technical, and organizational resources from which he or she may draw.

- establish consequences.

Because volunteers will vary in experience, abilities, and maturity, it is helpful to employ three progressive levels of delegation, depending on these factors:

• **Directing**. Provide a specific job description or list of duties, along with deadlines, to ensure his or her success. Most young, unproven volunteers (with low levels of maturity and skills) will appreciate this kind of oversight and guidance. After all, they want to succeed and not be left alone to sink or swim.

• **Coaching**. Allow him or her to design the plan and procedures, as you coach and advise along the way until the job is done. Use coaching anytime you work with people of moderate maturity and skill levels or with a high level of one and a low level of the other.

• **Delegating**. The job is his or hers. Because the maturity and skill levels are both high, you can trust this person to do the job right and on time. You have observed proven faithfulness over time.

In his book *The Seven Habits of Highly Effective People*, Stephen Covey writes:

> With immature people, you specify fewer desired results and more guidelines, identify more resources, conduct more frequent accountability interviews, and apply more immediate consequences. With more mature people, you have more challenging desired results, fewer guidelines, less frequent accountability, and less measurable but more discernible criteria.[9]

Trying to *direct* "high skill/high maturity" people will frustrate them. *Delegating* to "low skill/low maturity" people will most likely set you and them up for failure.

Give them the tools they need. I (Eric) was in Manchester, England, in 2003 for "Festival: Manchester"—a weeklong event sponsored by the Luis Palau Evangelistic Association. The event was divided into two parts—"On the Streets" and "In the Park." "On the Streets" consisted of five thousand young people from Western Europe working four to five hours each day painting buildings, removing graffiti, building soccer fields, restoring parks, planting daffodils, and so on. I've never seen youth work so hard—raking, shoveling, spading, weeding, painting, hauling. It was unbelievable. They were organized into 270 groups working on ninety different projects. During the week they removed more than sixty tons of rubbish from the city. The week culminated with "In the Park" in which over two nights, nearly fifty thousand people came out to join the "party," and hundreds of decisions were made for Jesus. Once again, good works paved the way for the good news.

The youth were able to work effectively because, partnering with the local police department, they were given high quality tools—the best rakes, shovels, brushes, gloves, and trash bags. Good tools leveraged their skills and gave them confidence. The best tools helped produce the best work.

Turn them into teachers. Peter Drucker says, "The most important way to develop people is to use them as teachers. Nobody learns as much as a good teacher. Selecting someone to be a teacher is also the most effective recognition."[10] Jay Lorenzen, of Campus Crusade for Christ's Military Ministry, points out that the ability to teach is the only skill among the character-laden list of qualifications for leaders in 1 Timothy 3:2-3; 2 Timothy 2:2, 24; and Titus 1:6-9.[11] Teaching, if it is done well, forces one to internalize principles so that they become one's own. Teaching forces one to articulate sentiments and experiences. Teaching identifies the values of the message with the values of the messenger. Give away your ministry by elevating others to tell their stories, to share their life-changing experiences, to pass on principles of externally focused ministry. Push others to the front, and expect them to contribute at a new level. In a healthy organization, everyone takes responsibility for learning, contributing, and leading.

Solicit their feedback. In her book *How to Mobilize Church Volunteers*, Marlene Wilson notes that "members seldom have a chance to express

- what they are good at;
- what they are tired of doing;
- what they don't like to do;
- what they want to learn;
- where they are being led to grow; and
- when they need a sabbatical."[12]

Make sure you put into place a tool or mechanism, such as a volunteer satisfaction survey, to get timely feedback from those who are serving. It is only through honest feedback that we can make mid-course corrections and serve those who are serving.

Funding

A major challenge in starting new ministries is money, but while money may be a key factor, it is not the only factor. No amount of money can make up for staff or volunteer leaders who lack character, integrity, or follow-through. Over time, people fund results, not intentions.

How a church spends its money on programming and staff is a reflection of what it believes is meaningful to God, the church, and the fulfillment of its mission. It's been said that our vision is only as big as that for which we are willing to raise money.

Our vision is only as big as that for which we are willing to raise money.

Funding Models

Three basic funding models may be used to support a church's externally focused ministry:

1. Externally focused ministry may be funded fully or nearly fully from the church budget. In this model, line items or budget categories pertaining to externally focused ministries are approved as part of the annual budget. This method has served Perimeter Church in Atlanta well in allocating hundreds of thousands of dollars annually to externally focused ministry.

2. Externally focused ministry, though housed within the church and sponsored by the church, may be treated as if it were a separate nonprofit

organization. Mariners' senior pastor Kenton Beshore discerned that people in his church had a higher capacity to give than they were giving to the church. So by treating Lighthouse Ministries as a separate organization and showcasing that ministry during a special weekend service, the church raises Lighthouse Ministries' entire budget in addition to what people already give to the church.

3. Externally focused ministry may be funded through the creation of a separate 501(c)(3) nonprofit organization with its own governance and funding strategies. Some churches have several independent nonprofit organizations that can accept government monies to support the nonreligious aspects of their endeavors, such as assisting with affordable housing, homeless shelters, and food banks. Using government money curtails the church's ability to *tell* the gospel—but not to live the gospel and show it to others.

A Closer Look

The Lake Avenue Foundation

Andy Bales of Lake Avenue Church in Pasadena, California, began the Lake Avenue Foundation—a separate 501(c)(3)—to better meet the needs of those he serves. When asked why he started a separate organization, Andy replied:

> We started it to raise outside resources to carry out the community work of the church because our "piece of the pie" at church was limited by mortgage, our million-dollar commitment to missions, etc. We wanted to greatly expand local transformation/development opportunities and felt that this was the best way to do it. Even though my first year as executive director of the foundation came right after 9/11, we expanded our budget from about $300,000 to $660,000 the first year and were able to expand our ministry, be accepted in wider circles, invited into the public schools, and receive grants from local businesses that would not normally give to a church while still carrying out kingdom work and sharing the gospel.[13]

Partnering

Partnering means to share in the efforts and outcomes of a venture. For a church to partner with other churches, organizations, or agencies means that it recognizes one of two things: (1) The job is way bigger than any one church can handle, or (2) God is already at work through other people of goodwill who care about what the church cares about. As we've shown throughout this book, it's often easier to form partnerships with existing groups than to spend the resources to start, staff, and fund something new. There's no reason to form a duplicate service or ministry if there's one already accomplishing its mission. Chances are that people from your congregation are already serving in it!

Imagine how great it would be if your church bulletin included not only a schedule of the men's and women's Bible study times, but a list of "Community Partner Ministries" as well. Maybe we can effectively show Christ's love to our city through agencies and mechanisms that already exist.

Partnering with churches or even secular organizations does not mean we must water down our beliefs or distinctives. We don't form our partnerships around our statements of faith or doctrine but rather our common love and commitment to our community. In Chapter 5 you may recall Rick's remark: "We may not always agree with other community service groups on the cause or the cure, but we do agree there is a problem." Even this minimum level of commonality can bring groups of people into partnerships.

> **We don't form our partnerships around our statements of faith or doctrine but rather our common love and commitment to our community.**

In March of 2003, many of our county's most evangelical churches were part of a one-day conference called "Restoring the Soul of Boulder County." The conference was sponsored by the Volunteer Connection and held at LifeBridge Christian Church. The speakers included leaders from several growing faith traditions in Boulder County—Christian, Jewish, Islamic, Baha'i, and Tibetan Buddhism (Boulder has the largest Tibetan Buddhism congregation in the U.S.). It was a wonderfully fascinating gathering as each speaker spoke about how his or her particular religion addresses social needs. As we planned the meeting, we all agreed that we did not have to compromise our individual beliefs to take part in this effort. We were not all going to stand on the platform and declare that we all believed the same thing and worshipped the same God. No! We were locking arms and hearts because of our shared love for and commitment to the community. To us there is no contradiction between standing in unity in meeting the needs of the community during the day and vigorously debating our belief systems at the university by night.

Partnering With Churches

Partnering with other churches is an effective way to maximize your efforts. In our community, First Presbyterian Church of Boulder hosts a program for the homeless called "Lamb's Lunch" at which church families share lunch, conversation, and the afternoon with homeless men and women in our community. One church provides the facility and invites other churches to simply join in.

Urban-Suburban Partnerships

Some suburban churches develop partnerships with urban churches and ministries. The great challenge of urban ministry in the U.S. is that the churches that are most in touch with the needs of people often have the least ability and capacity to meet those needs. Most urban churches are stretched to the limit. Urban pastors are often bi-vocational, fulfilling their calling by working two or more jobs. Churches in more affluent suburban areas often are resource rich (comparatively speaking) but out of touch with the needs of the under-resourced and disenfranchised. Urban-suburban partnerships can help close this gap.

Under the leadership of Pastor Alvin Bibbs, director of Extension Ministries at Willow Creek Community Church, the church has established forty "covenant partnerships" in the city of Chicago. A covenant partnership happens when a church or a parachurch organization is engaged in a ministry that Willow Creek also cares about. Willow Creek joins in—but in order to bless, not control. "This is relationship-driven; we engage with people before we contribute any money," says Alvin. Each partnership lasts for five years and is based on achieving the ministry's goals.

Although each partnership is relationally driven, Willow Creek provides laborers, expertise, strategic planning, and financial assistance. Each year Willow Creek provides grants in excess of $1 million to these forty partner ministries. The financial commitment is for three years of the five-year partnering commitment. After five years, these covenant partners become "friends of the ministry," and new ministries are adopted as covenant partners. This methodology allows those who had volunteered with the original covenant partner ministries to remain working with them, while new ministries are adopted for an expanding circle of volunteers.[14]

A Closer Look

Greenwood Community Church

Greenwood Community Church in Greenwood Village, Colorado, has had a fruitful eight-year partnership with His Love Fellowship (HLF)—an inner-city church in Denver. Pete Menconi, Greenwood's director of externally focused ministry, gives the following suggestions for successful urban-suburban partnerships:

1. Leaders of both ministries must be fully committed to the relationship. This means they are willing to spend time together (including spouses when possible) to get to know each other.

2. Any urban-suburban partnerships must be entered into on an equal basis. That is not about "haves" and "have-nots." Both churches have something to offer. For instance, a number of Greenwood men have been mentored and discipled by one of the HLF pastors. Greenwood leaders are mentoring HLF youth interns. This is a "win-win" relationship all the way around.

3. A healthy urban-suburban relationship takes time. It is a relationship...not a project. It must be allowed to unfold.

4. Initially it is helpful (and necessary) to create neutral venues for people from each church to meet one another. For example, Greenwood has sponsored a Cinco de Mayo celebration for five years at a neutral location where folks from both churches worked together. We have also hosted Thanksgiving outreaches,

a Christmas store, men's retreats, women's events, youth mentoring, mission trips to Mexico, golf tournaments, and golf outings.

5. Cross-cultural sensitivity and training are very helpful. While our society is becoming more diverse (and, interestingly, more homogeneous), a lot of people are still fairly clueless about others' lives and worldviews.

6. Always lead with relationships and not money.[15]

Parachurch Partnerships

Pastor Herb Reece was driving home with a carload of men from his fourth Promise Keepers gathering, and for the fourth time the men were clamoring to start a men's ministry in the church. Herb told the men, "Just show up at the church on Saturday at 8:00 a.m. with your rakes, drills, paintbrushes, and lawnmowers." Like Nehemiah, he did not tell them all the Lord had put on his heart. When the men showed up, Herb sent them in teams to the homes of the widows and single moms of his church. The men came back excited that they had "made the widow's heart sing" (Job 29:13) through their service.

This was the beginning of the New Commandment Men's Ministry, which has developed a threefold mission: (1) to make each widow or single mom feel as if Jesus himself has walked through the door, (2) to influence other believers in the church to minister to the distressed, and (3) to influence entire neighborhoods by serving and winning neighbors to Christ.

The strategy that has evolved is simple. Church teams of four to six men adopt one widow or single mom. Each team has a leader who is responsible for calling the woman each month and asking what needs to be done. The leader then tells his team what tools and materials will be needed. On the designated Saturday morning, the men meet from 7 to 8 o'clock over breakfast to pray, open the Scriptures, and go over last-minute details. From 8 to 10 o'clock, the men work at the house, ending in a time of prayer. The monthly three-hour commitment allows men to have a significant ministry without burdening or neglecting their own families.

Sometimes the men's work goes above and beyond simple maintenance.

Working with one of the single moms in the church, they discovered that her expenses were $200 a month greater than her income. They also discovered that she had an unfinished basement. The men pooled their resources and finished her basement, which she now rents out for $400 a month. These guys are making a difference.

One Saturday morning as they met at McDonald's for a brief devotion, prayer, and work assignments, an employee approached them and asked what they were doing every month. They explained, and the woman said that she also was a single mom with four kids. She asked if they would ever consider helping someone like her. She has since come to Christ and is active in the church.

What began as a ministry of mercy has become a wonderful evangelistic outreach. New Commandment Men's Ministry in Broomfield, Colorado, trains churches in practical men's ministry to "every widow, single mom, fatherless child, and distressed person in the church and beyond." This is the kind of parachurch ministry that makes a great church partner.

Secular Partnerships

As we've said, churches don't have to spend precious kingdom resources to duplicate what already exists. Let others spend their resources on infrastructure and staff. The church can provide what existing organizations need most—caring volunteers.

Although some churches question the advisability of partnering with secular organizations, remember the criteria: morally positive (they are doing good things) and spiritually neutral (they don't have a spiritual agenda of their own). It is difficult to support and provide volunteers for an organization that wants to promote its own beliefs, but you can be a part of a neutral group that invites those of multiple religious persuasions to the table.

A Closer Look

Biblical Examples

The Bible abounds with examples of how God used secular people in partnership with his people to fulfill his purposes. Jesus' view of acceptable partners may be broader than you think. In Mark 9:40, Jesus says, "Whoever is not against us is for us." He does not say, "Whoever is not for us is against us." In other words, we have the freedom to think of all good-hearted people as being on "our side." Joseph accomplished God's purpose with Pharaoh's resources (Genesis 41:41-43). Nehemiah's rebuilding and repopulating project was funded by Artaxerxes (Nehemiah 2:4-9). And Esther utilized her relationship with King Xerxes to carry out God's purpose (Esther 2:1-18).

There are many ways to utilize and augment existing resources. Instead of each congregation having its own food pantry, many churches partner with the local community food bank. Food is a neutral commodity. There is not a Christian box of corn flakes that competes with a secular brand. When needy people request food, congregations refer these folks to their partner ministry. And when hungry people have spiritual needs, the food bank can refer these people to their partner churches. In our own community, the local safe house for abused women regularly makes referrals to seven faith communities.

Working with what already exists may be a church's most underleveraged opportunity. Most human service agencies need what the church could readily supply—caring volunteers, financial support, and even facilities. The door is always open for servants wanting to help. It is often through serving shoulder to shoulder with unchurched volunteers that relationships leading to conversation around spiritual matters are created. These people are merciful but often don't know why. Could it be that although they don't know him, they are reflecting the image of their Creator? You may be the fortunate one to explain that good piece of news. Evangelistic opportunities arise out of our commitment to bring all of ourselves (including our spiritual selves) into all of the community. We don't leave any part of us at home.

With partnering of any kind, it is helpful to remember Alvin Bibbs' words regarding the partnering organization's relationship to the church's volunteers—"If we can hook 'em, you've got to reel them in."[16] In other words, the church makes the connection, but it is up to the partner ministry to give the volunteers a good experience in order to retain them.

Measuring

Many churches are frustrated because they have no measuring or accountability systems in place. Pat McMillan of Team Resources in Atlanta captures this frustration in the observation "Ministries that don't measure can neither rest nor worship."[17] Before you can really measure genuine progress, you must decide on a common language and common measurements.

Common language. It's amazing how much misunderstanding can surround the simplest words. So, to avoid misunderstanding, it's important to agree on certain key definitions. One of the church's most ambiguous words is *reached*. This is the term found in the annual report: "Our programs reached ten thousand people last year." What exactly does that mean?

Here is a list of terms that ministry partners should define in common:

- reach
- touch the lives of
- outreach
- exposures to the gospel
- gospel presentations
- decisions
- people served
- assimilated
- involved
- unchurched
- de-churched
- volunteers
- champions
- paid volunteers
- staff
- part-time staff
- ministry
- partnering (partner ministries)

Communication and data are meaningless unless we agree on common definitions. Because the culture and language of profit and nonprofit organizations are different, we must also acquire the ability to "translate" to the outside world, without ambiguity, what we do and what we are trying to achieve.

Common measurement. We must also decide with our ministry partners exactly *what, how,* and *when* we will measure, and then we must stick to it. Don't start measuring one thing this year and something else next year; if you do, you'll never have good, meaningful data. The Southern Baptists decided years ago how they would measure evangelism. They would measure baptisms—not "conversions" or "decisions." There is no ambiguity about whether a person has been baptized.

Good data tells you whether you are improving, declining, or plateauing. Good data provides the information necessary to plan and to decide what you will continue to fund and staff and what you must stop doing.

So what should you measure? **First, measure inputs**: how much of what resources you put toward your objectives and ultimately, your mission. For example, how many volunteers did you recruit, train, and deploy? How frequently did they serve? How many hours did they serve? How much money was budgeted, raised, and spent?

You can and should set goals regarding inputs (for example, to raise the number of volunteers in your church from 30 percent to 60 percent or to increase the number of community partner ministries from three to six). Measuring inputs defines what resources are put toward achieving outcomes, and this is only meaningful if it tells you how close you are to seeing your vision reach fruition.

At Willow Creek, the vision of the Extension Ministry is that "every fully devoted follower of Jesus Christ would model a lifestyle of compassion." Since the scope of the vision is "every fully devoted follower," the leaders of the church know exactly how far they have to go. In 2002 Willow Creek had 11,230 people engage in externally focused ministry that took compassion to the streets. Each of these people served 4.2 times during the year, giving five or more hours each time. They worked side by side with their covenant partners and friends of the ministry. Working in small groups or as families, they filled over two thousand backpacks with school supplies (and Bibles) as part of their effort to serve schools. Alvin Bibbs' goal is to increase the numbers serving, the hours they serve, the frequency of their service, and the depth of their service—moving people from acts of low-touch service toward "committed relational service."[18] Always measure against your mission.

Measuring inputs is necessary, but it is less than the full equation. You must also **measure outcomes, or results**, of your efforts and use of resources. Our inputs reflect our efficiency, but our outcomes reflect our effectiveness. We who work in the nonprofit sector always find it difficult to measure results. A business always has a tangible bottom line on its profit and loss statement, but what is our bottom line? Peter Drucker sheds light on this topic. He points out that the bottom line for all nonprofit organizations is always one thing: "changed human beings."[19] Hospitals exist to make sick people well; schools exist to educate the ignorant; churches exist to win the lost and build up the saints.

So how does the church measure changed lives? What are the measurable "expected outcomes" of the church's endeavors? Here's an example: If your people are involved in after-school tutoring, your expected outcome might be "to raise the reading level of those students who are reading below grade level to grade level or above." Begin by measuring how many were reading below grade level when the school year began (your current reality), and then measure how many were reading below grade level when the school year ended. For example, Willow Creek tracks two outcomes: the spiritual development of the volunteers and the changes in the community.

Because your mission is about expanding the kingdom of God, you should also measure how many people heard the gospel and how they responded. Remember, the church is about good deeds *and* good news.

Max De Pree, chairman emeritus of Herman Miller Inc., adds another factor that is difficult to quantify but is necessary to account for. In his book *Leading Without Power,* he writes, "Don't measure only what's easily measurable. We need to learn how to measure what's significant."[20] He goes on to say, "To measure does not always mean to quantify. I can certainly measure my love for my family, though I couldn't quantify it in a million years of trying."[21]

Something to **Think** About

If we are not measuring, we're just practicing.

Something to **Talk** About

1. This chapter discusses the challenges an externally focused church faces in the areas of staffing, funding, partnering, and measuring. Of these, what are the top two challenges facing your church?
2. Where could you find help in overcoming these challenges?
3. What are some of the benefits to your church of partnering with other organizations?
4. What are some of the pitfalls of partnering with other organizations?
5. How can you turn volunteers into teachers?

Something to **Act** Upon

Define the terms listed on page 193. Decide what, how, and when you will measure.

Sermon/**Lesson** Idea

Text: Nehemiah 2:1-18

Main Idea: The partnership between Nehemiah and Artaxerxes serves as a model for a partnership between people of faith and secular institutions.

Illustration: Potential partners in your community—Big Brothers, Big Sisters, Food Bank, Habitat for Humanity, and so on.

Action Point: Have a booklet printed describing twenty to thirty opportunities to partner with community ministries and human-resource organizations.

Endnotes

1. http://www.brainyquote.com/quotes/authors/w/winston_churchill.html

2. Dr. Howard Hendricks, former chaplain to the Dallas Cowboys, attributed this quotation to Tom Landry.

3. Erwin Raphael McManus, comments (conversation with Eric Swanson in 2002 and confirmed via e-mail in 2003).

4. See also Albert-László Barabási, *Linked* (New York: Plume, 2003), 3-4.

5. Dave Workman, comments (Cincinnati, OH: conversation with Eric Swanson, Vineyard Church, May 6, 2003).

6. Timothy J. Keller, *Ministries of Mercy: The Call of the Jericho Road* (Phillipsburg, NJ: P&R Publishing, 1997), 156.

7. Sue Mallory, *The Equipping Church* (Grand Rapids, MI: Zondervan, 2001), 37.

8. Peter F. Drucker, *Managing the Non-Profit Organization* (New York: HarperCollins Publishers, 1990), 148.

9. Stephen R. Covey, *The Seven Habits of Highly Effective People* (New York: Fireside, 1989), 179.

10. Drucker, *Managing the Non-Profit Organization,* 151.

11. Jay Lorenzen, comments (Allenspark, CO: "The Leader as Teacher" message delivered at Campus Crusade for Christ's Leadership Forum, October 22, 2003).

12. Marlene Wilson, *How to Mobilize Church Volunteers* (Minneapolis, MN: Augsburg Publishing House, 1983), 55-56.

13. Andy Bales, e-mail to Eric Swanson, September 30, 2003.

14. Alvin Bibbs, comments (South Barrington, IL: message at Willow Creek Community Church, July 23, 2003; and New York City: conversation with Eric Swanson, October 7, 2003).

15. Pete Menconi, e-mail to Eric Swanson, October 8, 2003. Used with permission.

16. Alvin Bibbs, comments (New York City: conversation with Eric Swanson, October 7, 2003).

17. Pat McMillan, comments (Estes Park, CO: meeting with the executive team of FamilyLife, October 1999).

18. Alvin Bibbs, comments (South Barrington, IL: seminar at Willow Creek Community Church, July 23, 2003).

19. Drucker, *Managing the Non-Profit Organization,* xiv.

20. Max De Pree, *Leading Without Power: Finding Hope in Serving Community* (San Francisco: Jossey-Bass, Inc., 1997), 15.

21. Ibid., 66.

chapter eleven

The **Best** Is Yet to **Come**

"The first question which the priest and the Levite asked [on the Jericho Road] was 'If I stop to help this man, what will happen to me?' But...the good Samaritan reversed the question: 'If I do not stop to help this man, what will happen to him?' "

—Martin Luther King Jr.

Perspective

There is a Taiwanese fable about a frog who lived in the bottom of a well. When the frog was thirsty, he drank a little bit of water from the well, and when he was hungry, he ate some insects that flew into the well. When he was tired, he lay on a little rock at the bottom of the well and looked up at the sky above him. To the little frog, the sky was a small circle of blue. He was very happy and satisfied, for this was the only world he had ever known.

One day a bird perched at the edge of the well. The little frog looked up and said, "Hello! Why don't you come down here and play with me? It's so pleasant down here. Look, I have cool water to drink and countless insects to eat. Come down!" But the bird responded with stories of an endless expanse of beautiful sky. The frog listened in disbelief then argued that the sky was small and round, for he had never been outside the well and seen the entire sky. The bird tried to coax the frog out of the well so he could see the sky, but the frog sat on his rock, convinced he was right. Eventually the bird flew away in frustration, and the frog was left alone to continue pondering his little patch of sky.

This story has a good ending. Eventually a yellow sparrow swooped into the well, put the frog on its back, and flew out of the dank well into the sunlight. For the first time, the frog saw flowers, trees, animals, mountains, and rivers. Finally the bird placed him on a lotus leaf in a beautiful pond where the frog enjoyed his days—never again to return to the well.

To a frog at the bottom of a well, the sky may be only a small circle of blue. But to a bird, the sky is vast and wonderful. In some ways they are both right. This fable is about perspective. In a world filled with other frogs, occasionally we need to listen to the birds.

Once a church moves outside its four walls—its well—and begins to experience the big world of ministry, things will never be quite the same. The well will seem small and provincial, safe but boring. The world of externally focused ministry will seem dangerous but exciting. Each church will have to decide to opt for safety or danger, boredom or adventure.

Understanding the Times

When David gathered to himself the tribes who would make him king, many were described as "brave warriors," "experienced soldiers," and those "ready for battle." Notable in the group, however, were the men from the tribe of Issachar. The text says nothing about their military prowess, but it does describe something about their approach to life: "[The] men of Issachar...understood the times and knew what Israel should do" (1 Chronicles 12:32a). They distinguished themselves from those around them by their understanding and perception of reality. And their perception of the present allowed them to act wisely; they knew just what to do. Knowing what to do seems to be correlated with understanding the times.

After complimenting some of his followers on their ability to forecast the weather, Jesus asked in Luke 12:56, "How is it that you don't know how to interpret this present time?" Jesus clearly wants us to know how to interpret the "present time." What are the impending trends? What should we be thinking about?

What's happening in evangelism? Dr. Thom S. Rainer, founding dean of the Billy Graham School of Missions, Evangelism, and Church Growth at the Southern Baptist Theological Seminary in Louisville, Kentucky, wrote a book called *The Bridger Generation*. In it, Rainer defines "bridgers" as the seventy-two million Americans born between 1977 and 1994. The bridgers are one of four generations of Americans who are identified by the year they were born and the times in which they grew up. The other generational groupings of the twentieth century are the "builders"—those born between 1910 and 1946, the "boomers"—those born between 1946 and 1964, and the "busters" (sometimes referred to as Generation X), who were born between 1965 and 1976.

The church has missed the harvest of an entire generation!

Drawing from his original research and that of others, he makes some startling observations. After detailing the cultural and spiritual influences of the bridgers, he concludes with his own observations of the spiritual condition of this generation: "In a recent and informal survey of 211 bridgers, only 4 percent responded that they were born-again Christians who had trusted in Christ alone for salvation."[1]

Here is a summary of his findings:

Estimated Proportion of Each Generation Reached for Christ

Builders—65 percent

Boomers—35 percent

Busters—15 percent

Bridgers—4 percent[2]

Those in youth ministry often make the statement that 80 percent of those who trust Christ as their Savior do so before the age of eighteen (and a large majority of those do so before fourteen). Juxtaposing these statistics, what do you conclude? If both sets of statistics are true, then we may safely conclude that the church has missed the harvest of an entire generation! (Of course fallacies often arise from analyzing statistics. Statisticians themselves often say, "If I had one foot in a bucket of ice and the other in the campfire, statistically speaking, I should be comfortable.")

Extrapolating these results thirty years into the future is profoundly sobering for the church. We are living off the energy and resources of the thirty-five and up crowd, totally unaware that those who follow them will be a much smaller group. In a recent discussion, one pastor was so deeply affected by these statistics that he said, "I'm tempted to turn the entire church into a huge youth group, and everybody else will just support the youth reaching their peers."

Yogi Berra said, "The future ain't what it used to be," and he is right. The future won't look like the past. We can't expect to get different results if we continue to do the same things.

We must also understand the effects of urbanization. At the turn of the twentieth century, 90 percent of Americans lived on farms. Today only 2 percent of Americans live on farms. Missions are no longer exclusively "to the nations" because many of the "nations" are moving to our cities. Rudy Carrasco of Harambee Christian Family Center tells about the good-hearted people in buses and church vans driving down the Golden State Freeway in Los Angeles, hurrying to get to Tijuana to reach Mexicans, but totally oblivious to the Mexicans and Latinos living in Los Angeles. Dr. Ray Bakke tells of one zip code in New York City that has people from 133 nations residing in it. Ray describes an exercise he does with his seminary students. They go into a supermarket in a major city and observe

> **Maybe we already know how to recognize where God is working in our environment and generation, but could we recognize the work of God in the next generation…among a different ethnic group?**

and "interpret" the store (in the same way one might observe and interpret the Scriptures) to find out what they can about the neighborhood. They talk to people and investigate the kinds of products the store sells. Where do the products come from? What language or languages are used in the signage? From these findings, the students are asked to form a picture of the neighborhood's composition. Then they go to a church in the neighborhood to do the same thing. Typically a sign out front (in English) reads:

9:30 a.m. Sunday School

11:00 a.m. Worship Service

Clearly, the neighborhood has changed, but the church hasn't. Then Ray asks, "How is it that the owners of the supermarket—without the Spirit of

God—can do a better job of understanding the people they are reaching than we, who have the Holy Spirit?"[3]

We need to understand the times so we know what to do. We need to understand where God is working so we can get in on it. Maybe we already know how to recognize where God is working in our environment and generation, but could we recognize the work of God in the next generation…among a different ethnic group?

Planned Abandonment

To move ahead, we must determine what we will leave behind. Jim Collins, co-author of *Built to Last* and author of *Good to Great*, tells about his desire to read more and the steps he took to reach that goal. He set up a reading room and bought the perfect chair for reading, a wonderful reading lamp, and all the books he wanted to plow through. But when he came home from work, he'd flop on the couch, flip on the television, and catch up on the news or the first quarter of *Monday Night Football*. Soon he'd be glued to the TV, and the books remained stacked on the chair in his reading room. Finally he got rid of the TV, and his reading accomplishments soared. He learned that it's not what you add to your life, it's what you abandon that will make the difference.[4] As you expand your externally focused ministries, what will you abandon? You can't continue to do everything.

As you expand your externally focused ministries, what will you abandon?

How many times does it take to create a church tradition? Only once…if it is successful. The methodologies that we currently use are the answers to the tough questions a previous generation (or two…or three) asked. The toughest programs to kill are those that are working. Remember that we organize around purpose, not around program or tactic. Every program that is effective today, no matter how good it is, has a life span. It eventually will lose momentum. We've got to be so in tune with God's purpose that our purpose isn't interrupted when a program runs out of steam.

When Hezekiah became king of Judah, one of his first acts was courageous. "He broke into pieces the bronze snake Moses had made, for up to that time the Israelites had been burning incense to it" (2 Kings 18:4b).

Generations earlier the Lord had told Moses to fashion a bronze snake and put it on a pole so if anyone was bitten by a snake, they could look at the bronze snake and live (Numbers 21:6-9). The tool that God had intended for one-time use had actually become an object of worship! Can you give away, abandon, break into pieces a program that God has used in the past? Can you master the skill of abandonment?

Find Ways to Be Useful

The early church created systems and mechanisms to ensure that the people would follow the teachings and practices of Jesus. Verses 1-4 of the twelfth chapter of the Didache (an anonymous, early second-century Christian treatise on morality and church practice) outline guidelines for dealing with strangers:

> Let every one that cometh in the name of the Lord be received, but afterwards ye shall examine him and know his character, for ye have knowledge both of good and evil. If the person who cometh be a wayfarer, assist him so far as ye are able; but he will not remain with you more than two or three days, unless there be a necessity. But if he wish to settle with you, being a craftsman, let him work, and so eat; but if he know not any craft, provide ye according to your own discretion, that a Christian may not live idle among you.[5]

Expanding on these guidelines, Clement of Alexandria (d. 215) wrote instructions for the church: "For those able to work, provide work; and to those incapable of work, be charitable."[6]

The early church was not only attractive for its mercy, but it also served as an agent of spiritual and societal transformation. The early church did not see engagement in community as optional but *essential* to its calling. To these brothers and sisters the term "externally focused church" would have been utterly redundant. The church, by definition, was externally focused!

Healing Waters International is a nonprofit organization in Golden, Colorado. Motivated by the fact that 3.4 million people die each year of water-related illnesses, this group installs water purification systems in churches in underdeveloped countries. These churches in turn provide affordable, pure drinking water to their communities at a fraction of the local prices. The people in these communities are not only being cured of waterborne diseases, but they are also seeing the church in a whole new light. What can your church offer your community? Child care? Life-skills training? Recovery workshops? What do you have of value in your church that's worth taking into the community?

Think and Act Counter-Culturally

Most of the time, Christians have the same response to life as everyone else. When the economy is strong and things are going well, we are fairly happy. When the economy hits a snag or tragedy strikes, we ride the roller coaster into the valley with everyone else. Perhaps the biggest opportunities for the church occur not in the best of times but the worst of times. In Chapter 6 we described how the early Christians hunkered down in the cities to look after victims of the plague. While everyone around them fled, the Christians decided to stay.

We should rejoice and be thankful during the good times, but during the downturns and tragedies perhaps we should ask ourselves, "What new opportunities does this event present to the church?" Churches that are thinking this way are reaching out to Muslim international students, are ministering to families of deployed soldiers, are engaged in job training, and are reaching out in myriad ways to others.

Positive Deviants

In the 1990s Jerry and Monique Sternin, staff members of Save the Children, responded to a request from the Vietnamese government to help fight malnutrition in the country's villages. Nearly half the country's children were malnourished. The Sternins had six months to produce results. They didn't have time to implement an outside solution. The answer to the problem had to lie within the villages themselves.

Drawing from research done by Marian Zeitlin at Tufts University, the Sternins applied the theory of "positive deviants" to their Vietnamese setting. In each of the four villages where they began working, they found parents whose children were well nourished and thriving but who had access to the same resources as those parents whose children were malnourished. If it could be discovered what the parents of the thriving children did that "deviated" (hence the term *deviants*) from the others, then those practices could be distilled and passed on to the others in the village. *Positive deviants* are those in every community who, using the identical resources, have discovered how to get better results than those around them.

The Sternins discovered that the "deviant" parents were straining tiny shrimp and crabs from the rice paddies and collecting sweet-potato greens to add to their staple diet of rice. These protein- and vitamin-rich foods, added to the carbohydrates in rice, allowed the children to thrive.

Armed with these findings, the Sternins went from four villages to sixteen villages and eventually reached 2.2 million Vietnamese people in 265 villages. The program has since been implemented by Save the Children in over twenty countries and has resulted in thousands of saved lives.[7]

In every under-resourced part of your community, some families and individuals are thriving even though they have access to the same resources as everyone else. What can you discover about what they are doing differently that others could apply? Are there churches in your community that are getting better results than your church is currently getting, without access to greater resources? What are they doing that you could apply to your setting? We don't have to be original to be effective. We can and should be committed to learning all we can from the mistakes and successes of others. The early bird may get the worm, but the second mouse gets the cheese.

The Power of Small Things

In 1987, Mike Hayes of Rochelle, Illinois, was a freshman at the University of Illinois, and he was trying to figure out how to pay for college. He came up with an innovative solution. He wrote to Chicago Tribune columnist Bob Greene, asking each of Mr. Greene's readers to send Hayes a penny. Greene took a liking to the idea and asked each of his several million readers to send Hayes a penny. Thousands responded. In less than a month, the "Pennies for Mike" fund contained 2.3 million pennies! Some readers who weren't content to send pennies sent in quarters, dimes, and nickels; some even sent checks. In the end Mike raised over $28,000, which paid for four years of college tuition (remember this was 1987).[8] Mike didn't ask for a lot, but he asked for a little from a lot of people. That was the secret of his success. Isn't that amazing? The church's greatest impact may not stem from asking for great things from a few people, but for many small things from a lot of people. Can you imagine how different our world would be if every Christian personally engaged in some form of outreach or service?

In Dallas one woman decided to make a difference for a homeless man and his wife who spent their nights at the Austin Street Shelter. The man was a skilled craftsman who whittled and carved five-foot walking sticks. Called Moses Sticks, each was artistically engraved with the Ten Commandments. This woman saw an immediate business opportunity and at the same time an opportunity to move this couple out of the shelter and into a place of their own. Soon a deal was struck. She became the man's "art agent," buying every walking stick he made. What was once a pastime has become a way to make a living. Since June of 1998, he and his wife have been off the streets and living in an apartment of their own. No government money was needed or asked for. This was simply one merciful person empowering a capable person in need.

> **The church's greatest impact may not stem from asking for great things from a few people, but for many small things from a lot of people.**

Today these Moses Sticks are possessed by the president of the United States as well as members of the clergy, politicians, business professionals, and art collectors all over the country.[9]

A Closer Look

We Can't Do Everything, but We Can All Do Something

Dennis drove by a certain trailer every day on his way to work. Sometimes he'd see the occupant propped against a tiller in his yard as he struggled to work the soil. He was thirty-two years old, but he'd never had a paying job. He was disabled. When he was nine, a doctor had given him a shot that had paralyzed him from the waist down. He would never walk again. The disability checks from the county and state allowed him to exist. He couldn't afford leg braces, so he had a welder make a strip of steel that he strapped to his legs to give them stability as he walked on crutches.

One day Dennis decided to stop and talk to the man. His name was Lee. Exceptionally cheerful in spite of his condition, he demonstrated no rancor toward the doctor or society. His body was disabled, but his soul was intact.

As Dennis talked to Lee, a friendship was born. One day Dennis brought Lee a used computer and said, "If you can learn to type, there may be a job for you in my company."

Lee learned to type, and just to make sure he'd arrive at the job interview on time, he practiced the long walk to the bus stop. He secured a job in the customer service and order procurement department. A few months later, Lee began learning how to drive. Prior to that, the only thing that Lee had driven was a riding lawnmower that he had used to cut lawns in the summer. Finally, after six months, Lee passed his driver's license test, and Lee and Dennis went looking for a truck. They found a perfect little red truck right before Christmas. Lee was so excited that he drove to Memphis just to see another town. He had never been out of the state at night.

Lee still works full-time and is also enrolled in college, making the dean's list on more than one occasion. One man helped another man...and both men will never be the same. We can't do everything, but we can all do something.

What Turns Intention Into Action?

In the 1960s, social psychologist Howard Levanthal wanted to see if he could persuade a group of seniors at Yale University to get tetanus shots. He formed two control groups. One group was given a seven-page booklet graphically showing the terrifying effects of tetanus—pictures of a child having a tetanus seizure and other tetanus victims with tracheotomies, catheters, nasal tubes, and so forth. The second group was given a booklet with toned-down language and no pictures. Both booklets announced that the university was offering free shots at the health center. The results were both predictable and surprising. The students who were given the more dramatic information were much more likely to say that they intended to be inoculated than those who were given the casual information. But one month later, a mere 3 percent of the students had actually gone to the health center for inoculations. Levanthal conducted the experiment a second time but with one key change. This time he included a map of the campus with the health center circled and listed the times the shots were available. This small change caused the response rate to take a dramatic jump. A month later, 28 percent of students had been inoculated—an equal number from each control group. The variable was not the level of urgency or gravity; it was the map and schedule.[10] When recruiting volunteers, one of the best things we can do is give people accurate, practical information about how and when they can get involved.

Many good-hearted people in your church would love to serve and minister, but they lack a mechanism to turn desire into action. They need to know how many are needed, when they are needed, and how long they will be needed. Biblical encouragement is good, but it is not sufficient to engage people in service. Encouragement must be accompanied by many, many opportunities. Service only happens when inclination meets opportunity.

> Many good-hearted people in your church would love to serve and minister, but they lack a mechanism to turn desire into action.

We Need People With Big Hearts and Big Brains

High-capacity, successful people understand and recognize the power of leverage as instinctively as the rest of us recognize the color blue. They hear an idea or potential solution or opportunity, and their brains immediately run the numbers to determine the outcome of the investment. They seem to know instinctively whether an undertaking is worth their time and effort. We will never capture the hearts and minds of these people by assigning them to ladle beef stew in a soup kitchen. They might do it one time, but that will be it. While ladling soup, they'll find themselves thinking, "I'd be better off donating the $200 I would earn if I invested this hour doing what I do best." We need to create high-capacity challenges for high-capacity people. The challenge for high-capacity people is not to discern how to more efficiently ladle soup, but to figure out why there are so many people in line for soup. High-capacity people don't ask, "How can we raise the money to start five new ministries?" Rather, they ask, "How can we start thirty new ministries without money?"

The best way to engage the hearts of high-capacity people is by engaging their minds around big challenges and ideas. Daniel H. Burnham, the architect who rebuilt Chicago after the Chicago fire and came up with the first comprehensive plan for an American city, said, "Make no little plans; they have no magic to stir men's blood and probably themselves will not be realized. Make big plans; aim high in hope and work, remembering that a noble, logical diagram once recorded will not die."

A few years ago, Don Harris began thinking about capital formation. He recognized that in the U.S. most net worth is vested in people's homes. Homeowners get better tax breaks than renters. Under most economic conditions, a home is one of the few appreciating assets. But Don realized that many people with full-time jobs and good credit are unable to obtain home loans because they are never able to save enough money for a down payment. Then Don noticed something else: Most sellers sell their homes for 3 to 7 percent below their original asking price. Putting these two pieces of information together, he began the Nehemiah Corporation (www.nehemiahcorp.org), built around a three-way virtuous cycle. Nehemiah Corporation *gives* potential homeowners (with good credit but no savings) 3 percent of the asking price under these conditions: Homeowners pay the asking price for the house, and the seller rebates 3 percent to Nehemiah Corporation! It's a brilliant solution that lay dormant until someone with a big brain cared about this issue so much that he wouldn't stop thinking about it until he came up with a solution. Since 1997, Nehemiah Corporation has assisted over 160,000 families by providing more than $626 million in down payment gift funds.

A Closer Look

Thousands of Free Wheelchairs

Years ago, Don Schoendorfer was in Morocco and saw something that would change his life and the lives of thousands of others. He saw a crippled woman dragging herself across a dirt road. Don realized that this woman represented countless people around the globe who crawl along the ground or wait for friends or loved ones to pick them up and carry them. Don saw what people had seen for centuries, but his training as a mechanical engineer triggered a different train of thought. What if he could design an inexpensive wheelchair, using mountain-bike wheels rather than standard wheelchair wheels, that could withstand the conditions of streets in developing countries? Don put together a prototype chair and placed it in the courtyard of Mariners Church in Irvine, California. Other engineers came by and added their improvements until the result was a lightweight, low-cost, practical design that could be built and delivered to any country in the world for under $42. This project so captivated Don that he quit his job and began Free Wheelchair Mission (FWM). Can you imagine the life changes Don has seen and the testimonies he has heard from people who one day were pulling themselves along the ground and the next day were mobile? FWM has distributed thousands of free wheelchairs in the name of Jesus to people in Afghanistan, China, Angola, India, and several other developing countries. People with big hearts and big intellectual capacity need to be thinking about the big problems of our world.

A Kingdom Assignment

In November of 2000, Pastor Denny Bellesi of Coast Hills Community Church in Aliso Viejo, California, did something that will reverberate for years to come. After preaching about the parable of the talents (Matthew 25:14-30), he asked one hundred people to come forward for a "Kingdom Assignment." As they came forward, he handed each of them a crisp one hundred dollar bill and told them to invest the money for the kingdom and in three months report the results. In February, volunteers reported how the money had been spent and multiplied on transforming lives, feeding hungry people, building churches, and scores of other God-directed ventures. Some felt this was the most significant thing they had ever done.[11] But there was more.

After the events of September 11, 2001, much of the charitable giving that in the past had gone to the community was sent to New York instead, which left the local food bank and other agencies dangerously low on resources. Denny preached about the rich ruler (Luke 18:18-30). He asked a thousand people in the church to each sell something for $100 and bring the money back to the church on Thanksgiving weekend. They collected over $100,000, which they distributed to local human-service agencies to meet basic needs such as food, clothing, and shelter for men, women, and children.[12] Talk about having an impact on the community!

But there was a third Kingdom Assignment. In the fall of 2002, Denny preached about the "least of these" (Matthew 25:31-46) and challenged two thousand people to each give ninety minutes over the next ninety days to whomever they considered to be the "least of these." Once again, the church deployed huge numbers of people into the community; meeting needs they had never met before. Denny and his wife, Leesa, have told their story on *Oprah* and have given all churches a great idea for having a sustainable impact on their communities.[13]

When a young entrepreneur in our community heard about the Bellesis' idea of investing talent, treasure, and time, his eyes lit up. He put up $50,000 to help launch the concept with a critical mass of churches in our community. These churches have modified the concept in a way that should create a cascading effect. After completing the second Kingdom Assignment, each church takes the equivalent of the money it was given in the first Kingdom Assignment and uses it as "seed money" to implement the first Kingdom Assignment in another church—with the stipulation that this church also do all three Kingdom Assignments, including seeding another church. And so the cycle should continue. This will most likely be the best investment this young businessman will ever make.

In June 2003, Pastor Tom Shirk of Calvary Bible Church in Boulder challenged his congregation with its first Kingdom Assignment. After preaching on the parable of the talents, he asked fifty people from each service to come forward for a Kingdom Assignment. "For some of you," he said, "this will be the most important thing you have ever done in your entire life." People streamed forward, and Tom handed each of them a hundred-dollar bill. As the money ran out, a man in the congregation came forward and thrust a handful of hundred dollar bills into Tom's hand so that everyone who wanted to participate could take part in this assignment. Then, as in the parable of the talents, Tom told them to "go multiply it for the kingdom." The only stipulations were that the participants had to multiply the money; give it to something that would expand God's kingdom; and, three months later, report how they'd invested it. One family took its $100 and sponsored a dog wash. They made $1,300 and donated the money to the safe house for battered women. Another family planted a garden and sold vegetables. One eleven-year-old boy asked for a dollar, made up fliers advertising his willingness to do yardwork that summer, and raised $273, which he donated to the "lost boys of Sudan" who live in Boulder. In all, Calvary turned $11,000 into over $50,000 in three months. This money was then given to individuals and causes the participants believed in—the food bank, the safe house for battered women, support for missionaries, Bibles, and so on. People began to experience the joy and adventure of stewardship.

In September 2003, after a message preached about the rich ruler who refused to sell his treasure (Luke 18:18-30), members at Calvary were challenged with another Kingdom Assignment. Two hundred people accepted the challenge to sell a "treasure" worth at least $100. In some cases, the treasure might be a hindrance to a more authentic walk with God. In other cases, the treasure might be something participants had lying around their houses. The money was to be collected around Thanksgiving and collectively distributed to three agencies that serve the poor in Boulder County.

The response was remarkable. One man sold his Rolex watch; another sold a big-screen TV. One family committed money from a timeshare vacation home that, along with over twenty other timeshares in the same complex, had been on the market for three years. Only one had been sold in the previous year, but this family's timeshare sold.

Altogether, these two hundred people raised more than $87,000. Of this, more than $78,000 was given to the three human-service agencies. When Pastor Tom Shirk, accompanied by a couple of staff members, presented the checks to the executive directors of the agencies, all three cried tears of gratitude, overwhelmed by the love and grace of God shown through a local church. Calvary is using the remaining $8,700 as seed money to start the first Kingdom Assignment in two other churches in Boulder.

Of this experience, one of the interns at Calvary wrote,

On my end, the Kingdom Assignments have renewed the boldness and peace I have in proclaiming Christ. God has blessed me with the opportunity to share the assignments with dozens of non-Christian friends and family. On many of these occasions, a friend or family member would ask why we are doing these assignments, or some other question that provided an immediate segue into the gospel message. Many seeds have been planted, hard ground has been sown, and planted seeds have been watered. Among other things, I am thankful that such assignments provide immediate avenues to a positive gospel presentation. They allow us to discuss real life experiences, which include the motives of Christ, and do so in a generally non-threatening way to the non-Christian.

From another church that completed the second Kingdom Assignment, one pastor wrote,

> Yesterday, my entire staff went together and delivered the checks. It was a powerful time as well...We took a tour of each place and then asked to pray for their agencies. God was really working, and bridges were built. Two of the people are coming to church this Sunday. It should be mandatory for churches to be invested in their cities this way!

High-capacity people need high-capacity challenges.

Change the Conversation

Put two pastors in a room together, and you can bet that within the first five minutes someone will ask, "What are you runnin' these days?" That's pastor talk for "How large is your attendance?" or "What size is your church?" Maybe the conversation needs to change to "Tell me about the difference your church is making in your community." If the other pastor starts mentioning numbers of people attending Sunday school

It's not about size; it's about impact.

or worship services, respond by saying something such as "Oh, I'm sure people love listening to your teaching, but what's happening in the community because of your church?"

It's not about size; it's about impact. Can you imagine the difference it would make if the more than 340,000 churches in North America all measured their effectiveness by external measures (impact on communities) rather than internal measures (attendance)? Can you imagine the difference it would make if every church around the world did the same?

We've Got to Take Some Risks

It would be great if everything we did were risk-free. It would be great if every dollar we spent resulted in miraculous stories of conversion, changed lives, and societal transformation. But it won't. It would be great if every person who left a secular job or retired early to meet the needs of people would be wildly successful. But that won't happen either. We will have our share of failures and setbacks.

The risk-takers in the marketplace—the "angel" investors and those who capitalize the early stages of businesses—move forward with the hope that one of every eight or ten investments pays off big and makes up for their losses. Their cavalier attitude is to be envied. We like to play it safe. We are too fearful. Eric's wife defines *fear* as the "anticipation of loss." What if we removed "loss" from the equation? In the parable of the talents (Matthew 25:14-30), the man who was paralyzed by fear and played it safe was soundly rebuked. It was the risk-takers, whose only fear was doing nothing, who multiplied the talents for the Master. When we stand before the Lord, the last thing we want to say to him is "Lord, I was afraid, so I…"

Do You Want to Get Well?

"Do you want to get well?" asked Jesus (John 5:6b). What a strange question for a perfectly healthy person to ask someone who had been an invalid for thirty-eight years!

In actuality, Jesus asked a very good question. I (Rick) have been in the people business for more than twenty-five years. I can't begin to tell you how many people have told me in one way or another that they would like to get well. They want their marriages to improve. They want to get over their addictions. They want their hearts to be healed. They would like to get well. I find myself asking, "Really? Do you really want to get well?"

A version of the invalid's response to Jesus' question has been repeated to me again and again. In essence, the invalid said, "I would if I could, but I cannot, so I am not. It isn't my fault." If you want to get well, things will have to change. The lifestyle to which you are accustomed will be different if you are well. Your friendships may need to change. Your habits will almost certainly have to change if you are going to be well. Do you really want to get well?

We all need to answer this question individually. Every church needs to answer this question as well. If we are going to get well, if our churches are going to get better, then some change is likely. Our lives are likely to be disturbed if we allow the One who can heal to lead.

The Best Is Yet to Come

In this book we've described some of the ways God is moving the church beyond the four walls of the building and into the community. And we've described some of the results: People are coming to faith, lives are being changed, and Christians are growing. But we really believe that the best years for the church are still ahead, and the best ideas have yet to be invented. The challenges and opportunities are too massive to rely on old, tired methodologies.

To create a different future is going to take leaders with the vision to see, the passion to feel, and the courage to do. These leaders must keep pressing forward despite inevitable squalls, adjusting the rudder and the sail as they go. "The voyage of the best ship is a zigzag line of a hundred tacks," according to Emerson.[14] Sometimes it may seem that you are not making progress, but you are. You are learning; you are growing. You are becoming more useful for the kingdom. After all, you are simply the helmsman, not the Captain, of this ship. You may not have a map, but you do have a compass. This is about the journey and adventure more than the destination. This is really about the kingdom, not programs. It's about relationships, not numbers. It's about changed lives, not endless activity. And you have your mates—those kindred spirits whose hearts beat with yours. Your provisions for the journey may be sparse, but real leaders have the ability to create something that doesn't exist...with resources they don't have. If that describes what you are trying to do, then you are in the right position. We encourage you to go forward, knowing that God meets us when we step out in faith. He reveals solutions as we go; we mustn't wait to act until we have all the answers.

We're glad you've joined the journey.

Something to **Think** About

We anticipate a time in the not-so-distant future when people will marvel that the church was once *not* externally focused and *externally focused church* is a redundant term.

Something to **Talk** About

1. Of all that your church is currently doing, what should it abandon in order to become more externally focused?
2. How can you help turn intention into action in deploying people into ministry and service?
3. What ideas from this chapter present the most potential for your church?

Something to **Act** Upon

Change the conversation. From this point on, refrain from asking others, "How big is your church?" Instead say, "Tell me about the impact your church is having on your community."

When confronted with a ministry decision, what would change if, for one year, you would ask yourself, "What would Jesus do?"

Sermon/**Lesson** Idea

Text: 1 Chronicles 12:32a

Main Idea: One of the key tasks of leaders is to understand the times so they know what to do.

Illustrations: Jesus said to the people of his day, "You know how to interpret the appearance of the earth and the sky. How is it that you don't know how to interpret this present time?" (Luke 12:56).

Current trends and various things people are doing to take advantage of them.

Progress report on the impact your church is currently having as a result of its external focus.

Action Point: Introduce the concept of accepting a Kingdom Assignment.

Endnotes

1. Thom S. Rainer, *The Bridger Generation* (Nashville, TN: Broadman and Holman Publishers, 1997), 165.
2. Ibid., 169.
3. Raymond Bakke, lecture (Dallas, TX: October 1, 2003).
4. Jim Collins, "Pulling the Plug," Inc. magazine (March 1997), 76-77.
5. http://www.ocf.org/OrthodoxPage/reading/St.Pachomius/Liturgical/didache.html
6. Adolf Harnack, *The Expansion of Christianity in the First Three Centuries, vol. 1* (Eugene, OR: Wipf and Stock Publishers, 1998), 218.
7. David Dorsey, "Positive Deviant," Fast Company magazine (December 2000).
8. http://www.snopes.com/college/admin/cent.asp
9. Susan Nowlin, "An Unexpected Ministry, An Unexpected Friendship," PCPC Witness, a publication of Park Cities Presbyterian Church (August 2000), 10.
10. Malcolm Gladwell, *The Tipping Point* (Boston: Little, Brown and Company, 2000), 96-97.
11. Denny and Leesa Bellesi, *The Kingdom Assignment* (Grand Rapids, MI: Zondervan, 2001), 12-13.
12. Denny and Leesa Bellesi, *The Kingdom Assignment 2* (Grand Rapids, MI: Zondervan, 2003), 22-23, 35, 112.
13. KingdomAssignment.com
14. Ralph Waldo Emerson, as quoted in *How to Change the World* by David Bornstein (Oxford, England: Oxford University Press, 2004), 120.

Appendix

Scriptures Revealing God's Heart for the Poor, the Needy, Widows, Orphans, and Aliens

Exodus
20:9-10; 22:21; 22:22-23; 23:6; 23:11

Leviticus
19:10; 19:33-34; 23:22; 25:35

Numbers
15:15-16

Deuteronomy
10:17-19; 14:28-29; 15:4; 15:7; 15:11; 16:14; 24:10-15; 24:17-21; 26:12-13; 27:19

1 Samuel
2:8

Esther
9:22b

Job
20:10; 22:8-10; 29:11-13; 30:25; 31:16-23; 31:31-32; 34:19

Psalms
14:6; 68:5; 68:10; 74:21; 82:2-4; 109:16; 112:9a; 113:7-8; 140:12; 146:7-8; 146:9

Proverbs
10:4; 10:15; 13:23; 14:20-21; 14:31; 19:17; 21:13; 22:2; 22:9; 22:16; 22:22-23; 28:8; 28:27; 29:7; 29:14; 31:8-9; 31:20

Isaiah
1:17; 10:1-2; 11:4a; 25:4a; 32:7; 58:6-7; 61:1

Jeremiah
5:28b; 7:5-7; 22:3; 22:15b-16

Ezekiel
16:49; 22:29; 47:22

Amos
5:11-12

Zechariah
7:9-10

Malachi
3:5

Matthew
5:3; 6:2-3; 19:21; 25:34-40

Mark
12:42-43; 14:7

Luke
4:18; 12:33; 14:13-14; 18:22; 19:8

Acts
4:34-35; 9:36; 10:31; 24:17

Romans
15:26

1 Corinthians
13:3

Galatians
2:10

1 Timothy
5:3-4; 5:16

James
1:27; 2:1-6a

Scriptures Concerning
Good Works and Good Deeds

Matthew
5:16

2 Corinthians
9:8

Ephesians
2:8-10

Philippians
1:6; 2:12b-13

Colossians
1:10

2 Thessalonians
2:16-17

1 Timothy
2:10; 5:10; 5:25; 6:18

2 Timothy
3:16-17

Hebrews
10:24; 13:20-21

James
2:14; 3:13

1 Peter
2:12

*As an extension of
our men's giving basket
ministry, we are forming
a group of those interested
in feeding the hungry
in our community.
Interested? Check the
box on the connect card*

Resources

Atkinson, Donald A., and Charles Roesel. *Meeting Needs, Sharing Christ.* Nashville, Tenn.: Lifeway Christian, 1995.

Bakke, Raymond. *A Biblical Word for an Urban World.* Valley Forge, Pa.: Board of International Ministries, American Baptist Churches in the U.S.A., 2000.

Bakke, Raymond. *A Theology as Big as the City.* Downers Grove, Ill.: InterVarsity Press, 1997.

Barabási, Albert-László. *Linked.* New York: Plume, 2003.

Barnett, Matthew. *The Church That Never Sleeps.* Nashville, Tenn.: Thomas Nelson Inc., 2000.

Belasco, James A. and Ralph C. Stayer, *Flight of the Buffalo: Soaring to Excellence, Learning to Let Employees Lead.* New York: Warner Books, 1993.

Bellesi, Denny and Leesa. *The Kingdom Assignment.* Grand Rapids, Mich.: Zondervan Publishers, 2001.

Bellesi, Denny and Leesa. *The Kingdom Assignment 2.* Grand Rapids, Mich.: Zondervan Publishers, 2003.

Bornstein, David. *How to Change the World: Social Entrepreneurs and the Power of New Ideas.* New York: Oxford University Press, Inc., 2004.

Bosch, David Jacobus. *Transforming Mission: Paradigm Shifts in Theology of Mission.* Maryknoll, N.Y.: Orbis Books, 1991.

Buford, Bob. *Halftime: Changing Your Game Plan From Success to Significance.* Grand Rapids, Mich.: Zondervan Publishers, 1997.

Campolo, Tony. *Revolution and Renewal.* Louisville, Ky.: Westminster John Knox Press, 2000.

Carle, Robert D., and Louis A. Decaro Jr., ed. *Signs of Hope in the City.* Valley Forge, Pa.: Judson Press, 1999.

Collins, James C., and Jerry I. Porras. *Built to Last: Successful Habits of Visionary Companies.* New York: Harper Business, 1994.

Conn, Harvie M. *Evangelism: Doing Justice and Preaching Grace.* Grand Rapids, Mich.: Zondervan Publishers, 1982.

—. *The Urban Face of Mission.* Phillipsburg, N.J.: P&R Publishing Company, 2002.

Connolly, Mickey, and Richard Rianoshek. *The Communication Catalyst.* Chicago: Dearborn Trade Publishing, 2002.

Cymbala, Jim. *Fresh Wind, Fresh Fire.* Grand Rapids, Mich.: Zondervan Publishers, 1997.

De Pree, Max. *Leading Without Power: Finding Hope in Serving Community.* San Francisco: Jossey-Bass, Inc., 1997.

Dennison, Jack. *City Reaching: On the Road to Community Transformation.* Pasadena, Calif.: William Carey Library, 1999.

Drucker, Peter F. *Managing the Non-Profit Organization.* New York: HarperCollins Publishers, 1990.

Dudley, Carl S. *Next Steps in Community Ministry.* Herndon, Va.: The Alban Institute Inc., 1998.

Easum, William M., and Dave Travis. *Beyond the Box.* Loveland, Colo.: Group Publishing, 2003.

Emerson, Michael O., and Christian Smith. *Divided by Faith: Evangelical Religion and the Problem of Race in America.* New York: Oxford University Press, 2000.

Flake, Floyd. *The Way of the Bootstrapper: Nine Action Steps for Achieving Your Dreams.* New York: HarperCollins Publishers, 1999.

Gallup, George Jr., and Michael D. Lindsay. *Surveying the Religious Landscape: Trends in U.S. Beliefs.* Harrisburg, Pa.: Morehouse Publishing, 1999.

Gladwell, Malcolm. *The Tipping Point: How Little Things Can Make a Big Difference.* Boston: Little, Brown and Company, 2000.

Harnack, Adolf. *The Expansion of Christianity in the First Three Centuries, Volumes 1 & 2.* Eugene, Ore.: Wipf and Stock Publishers, 1998.

Harper, Nile, ed. *Urban Churches: Vital Signs; Beyond Charity Toward Justice.* Grand Rapids, Mich.: Wm. B. Eerdmans Publishing Company, 1999.

Hugen, Beryl, ed. *Christianity and Social Work: Readings on the Integration of Christian Faith and Social Work Practice.* Botsford, Conn.: North American Association of Christians in Social Work, 1998.

Hunter, George G. *The Celtic Way of Evangelism: How Christianity Can Reach the West…Again.* Nashville, Tenn.: Abingdon Press, 2000.

Kallestad, Walt. *Turn Your Church Inside Out.* Minneapolis: Augsburg Fortress Publishers, 2001.

Keller, Timothy J. *Ministries of Mercy: The Call of the Jericho Road.* Phillipsburg, N.J.: P&R Publishing, 1997.

Kretzmann, John P., and John L. McKnight. *Building Communities From the Inside Out.* Chicago: ACTA Publications, 1997.

Lewis, Robert. *The Church of Irresistible Influence.* Grand Rapids, Mich.: Zondervan Publishers, 2003.

Lincoln, Eric C., and Lawrence Mamiya. *The Black Church in the African American Experience.* Durham, N.C.: Duke University Press, 1990.

Linthicum, Robert. *City of God, City of Satan.* Grand Rapids, Mich.: Zondervan Publishers, 1991.

Magnuson, Norris. *Salvation in the Slums.* Metuchen, N.J.: The Scarecrow Press, Inc., 1977.

Mallory, Sue. *The Equipping Church.* Grand Rapids, Mich.: Zondervan Publishers, 2001.

McManus, Erwin Raphael. *An Unstoppable Force.* Loveland, Colo.: Group Publishing, 2001.

Nalebuff, Barry, and Ian Ayres. *Why Not? How to Use Everyday Ingenuity to Solve Problems Big and Small.* Boston: Harvard Business School Press, 2003.

Perkins, John, ed. *Restoring At-Risk Communities: Doing It Together and Doing It Right.* Grand Rapids, Mich.: Baker Books, 2000.

—. *Beyond Charity.* Grand Rapids, Mich.: Baker Books, 1993.

Rainer, Thom S. *The Bridger Generation.* Nashville, Tenn.: Broadman and Holman, 1997.

Sherman, Amy L. *Reinvigorating Faith in Communities.* Indianapolis: Hudson Institute, 2002.

—. *Restorers of Hope.* Wheaton, Ill.: Crossway Books, 1997.

Sider, Ronald J., Philip N. Olson, and Heidi Rolland Unruh. *Churches That Make a Difference: Reaching Your Community With Good News and Good Works.* Grand Rapids, Mich.: Baker Books, 2002.

Sjogren, Steve. *101 Ways to Reach Your Community.* Colorado Springs, Colo.: NavPress, 2001.

—. *Conspiracy of Kindness.* Ann Arbor, Mich.: Servant Publications, 1993.

Stark, Rodney. *The Rise of Christianity.* San Francisco: HarperCollins Publishers, 1997.

Stringer, Doug. *Somebody Cares.* Ventura, Calif.: Regal Books, 2001.

Wilson, Marlene. *The Effective Management of Volunteer Programs.* Boulder, Colo.: Volunteer Management Associates, 1996.

—. *How to Mobilize Church Volunteers.* Minneapolis: Augsburg Fortress Publishers, 1990.

—. *You Can Make a Difference.* Boulder, Colo.: Volunteer Management Associates, 1993.

Woodson, Robert L. *The Triumphs of Joseph: How Today's Community Healers Are Reviving Our Streets and Neighborhoods.* New York: Free Press, 1998.